75 Lace Crochet Motifs

75 Lace Crochet Motifs

Traditional designs with a contemporary twist, for clothing, accessories, and homeware

Caitlin Sainio

St. Martin's Griffin
New York

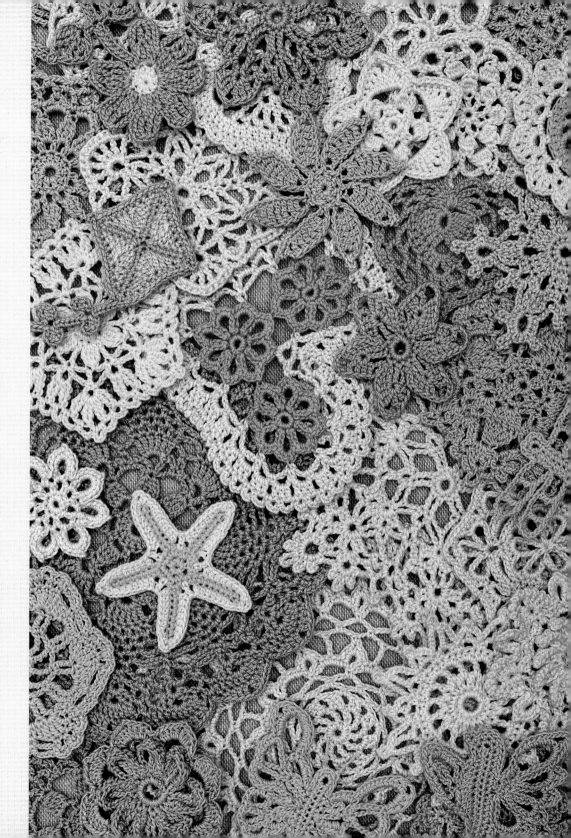

75 Lace Crochet Motifs

A Quarto Book
Copyright © 2014 Quarto Inc.
All rights reserved.

Printed in China. For information, address
St. Martin's Press, 175 Fifth Avenue, New
York, N.Y. 10010.

www.stmartins.com

Library of Congress Cataloging-in-
Publication Data
Available Upon Request

ISBN: 978-1-250-05911-6

St. Martin's Griffin books may be
purchased for educational, business, or
promotional use. For information on bulk
purchases, please contact Macmillan
Corporate and Premium Sales Department
at 1-800-221-7945 extension 5442 or write
specialmarkets@macmillan.com.

First Edition: January 2015

10 9 8 7 6 5 4 3 2 1

Conceived, designed, and produced by
Quarto Publishing plc
The Old Brewery
6 Blundell Street
London N7 9BH

QUAR.LCMM

Senior Editor: Victoria Lyle
Art Editor: Emma Clayton
Designer: Joanna Bettles
Photographer: Phil Wilkins
Pattern Checker: Therese Chynoweth
Proofreader: Ruth Patrick
Illustrator: Kuo Kang Chen
Indexer: Helen Snaith
Art Director: Caroline Guest
Creative Director: Moira Clinch
Publisher: Paul Carslake

Color separation in Singapore by
Pica Digital Pte Limited

Printed in China by 1010 Printing
International Limited

Contents

Foreword

As a crochet designer, I'm occasionally asked about my design process—where do all of these patterns come from? At its core, my creative process hasn't changed much, since the days when a new set of markers and a thick pad of paper would occupy me for hours. I draw my pictures with thread now, but my sources of inspiration are similar. Sometimes I set out to create a particular object that happens to be on my mind. Other times, a group of stitches reminds me of a feather, or a flower petal, or an ice crystal, and I build a pattern around that shape. Finally, many of my favorite geometric patterns arise from the crochet equivalent of doodling: I start from a foundation ring and add whatever stitches cross my mind, until the design seems finished.

This book includes "crochet drawings" of all of these types. There are summery sea creatures that I crocheted while fantasizing about beach vacations, in the coldest months of a very long winter. There are birds that came about after stitch patterns reminded me of wings. And there are designs that started as absent-minded doodles, and turned into beautiful geometric blocks. Each was, in one way or another, a happy surprise to me, when it was finished. I hope that you'll share my happiness (and perhaps my surprise), as you make these motifs, and use them in projects of your own.

Caitlin Sainio

Caitlin Sainio

About This Book

Basics of Crochet

The book begins with basic crochet information about equipment, symbols, abbreviations, and terminology, as well as some notes on how to work the key stitches featured in the book. If you are new to crochet or just need a refresher, you will find all of the know-how you need to get started.

Motif Collection: Selector

The Motif Collection begins by displaying the 75 beautiful designs that feature in this book. Flip through this colorful visual guide, select your design, and then turn to the relevant page of instructions to create your chosen piece.

In the selector the motifs are grouped into themes.

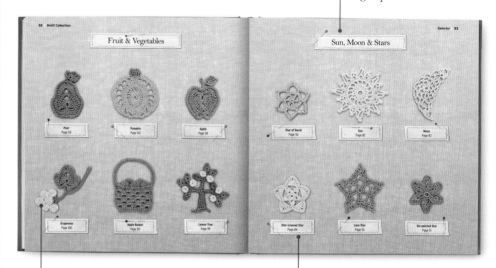

The visual selector shows photographs of all the motifs in the book at actual size.

The name and page number for the instructions enable easy navigation through the book.

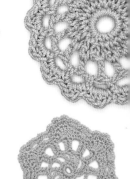

Motif Collection: Instructions

The instructions feature a chart, finished photograph, and written instructions. This is so that you can use either method or, better still, combine both.

The motifs are categorized by level of difficulty: beginner, intermediate, advanced.

Full instructions are provided for each motif.

Charts for each design act as a visual accompaniment to the written instructions.

A photograph shows the motif at actual size.

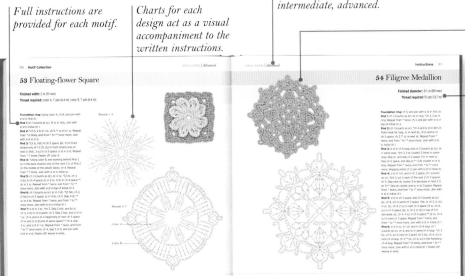

The finished dimensions and the yarn required are given.

The symbols used in the chart are listed.

Projects

The beauty of these motifs is that they can all be used to embellish a number of items, from garments and gifts to home accessories. This chapter presents a selection of ideas to inspire and encourage you to use the featured designs in a variety of ways–on their own, grouped, or joined together.

A close-up photograph of each project shows in detail how the item has been made and put together.

1 Basics of Crochet

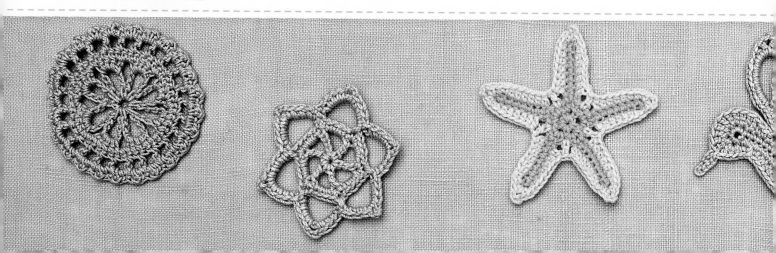

The book begins with basic crochet information about equipment, symbols, abbreviations, and terminology, as well as some notes on how to work the key stitches featured in the book. If you are new to crochet or just need a refresher, you will find all of the know-how you need to get started.

Before You Begin

Tools and materials

One of the attractions of crochet motifs is that they do not require a large collection of specialized tools or materials. Select a steel hook and a ball of crochet thread, gather a few common household supplies, and you'll be ready to begin.

Crochet hooks

For crocheting in thread, you will need a small, steel crochet hook. The patterns in this book were developed using a size 7 (1.65 mm) hook. Thread thicknesses vary, as do the gauges of individual crocheters, so any hook size recommendation should be taken as a starting point only. For the purposes of these motifs, the correct hook to use is the one that allows you to work most comfortably with your chosen thread.

Crochet thread

Lace motifs are usually crocheted from cotton crochet thread, which comes in sizes from 3 to 100, with higher numbers indicating finer threads. The patterns in this book were developed using size 10 thread. Experiment with finer threads and smaller hooks to create smaller, lighter-weight motifs. You may also wish to try other materials, such as lace-weight yarns or embroidery floss, for beautiful and sometimes surprising results.

Scissors

A small, sharp-pointed pair of scissors is especially helpful for clipping thread ends.

Straight pins

Use straight pins made from stainless steel, nickel-plated brass, or another rust-proof material, to hold your motif in position during blocking. It is a good idea to test the pins before use, to ensure that they won't stain your motifs. To do this, pin some to a piece of white fabric or a small crochet sample, dampen it with your choice of stiffener, let it dry, and then check for rust spots or stains.

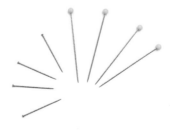

Symbols and abbreviations

Here you will find information on the abbreviations, symbols, and terminology used in the Instructions chapter.

Basic symbols and abbreviations

Symbol	Name	Abbreviation
⬯	Chain	*ch*
●	Slip stitch	*sl st*
+	Single crochet	*sc*
T	Half double crochet	*hdc*
⊤	Double crochet	*dc*
⊤	Treble	*tr*
⊤	Double treble	*dtr*

∪	Work in the single front strand of the stitch below.
∩	Work in the single back strand of the stitch below.
➤	An arrowhead indicates the beginning of a row or round where this is not immediately apparent.

Increases

Symbols joined at the base show stitches worked in a single stitch or space to make an increase. They are usually described as "work so many stitches in the next stitch," or at the beginning of a row "work so many stitches in the stitch below."

 2-st sc increase

 2-st dc increase

 3-st dc increase

 2-st tr increase

 3-st tr increase

Decreases

Symbols joined at the top show stitches gathered into one stitch to form a decrease. Each stitch of the group (dc, tr, etc., according to the symbol) is made without working the last wrap (a wrap is: yarn round hook then pull yarn through loop). This leaves one loop on the hook for each incomplete stitch plus the original loop. The decrease is completed by taking the yarn round the hook and then pulling the yarn through all loops on the hook.

 2-st hdc decrease

 2-st dc decrease

 3-st dc decrease

 2-st tr decrease

 3-st dtr decrease

Clusters

A cluster is made exactly like a decrease (see left) except that the stitches are all worked in a single stitch or space before being gathered together at the top.

 2-st dc clusters

 3-st dc cluster

 2-st tr cluster

 3-st tr cluster

 4-st tr cluster

 2-st dtr cluster

Additional pattern notes

- In all of the patterns in this book, motif dimensions and thread yardage estimates assume the use of size 10 thread and a size 7 (1.65 mm) hook.

- Asterisks (* **) indicate material to be repeated, with starting and ending points:

Repeat from * repeat all instructions that you've been given, starting with the last *.

Repeat from * to ** repeat the instructions between the last * and the ** that follows it.

- In motifs, it is common for a group of stitches to be repeated several times, and then partially repeated again.

Repeat from * 4 times, and from * to ** once more repeat all instructions, starting at the last *, 4 times. Then begin a fifth repetition, but stop when you get to the **.

Crochet Refresher Course

For readers who are new to crochet (and those who could use a review), this section provides instruction on the stitches used in this book. If you've never crocheted before, start by working the stitches with a large crochet hook in medium-weight yarn. Once you are comfortable with them, switch to thread.

Holding the hook and yarn

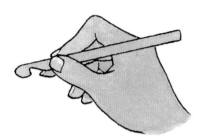

1 Holding the hook as if it were a pen is the most widely used method. Center the tips of your right thumb and forefinger over the flat section of the hook.

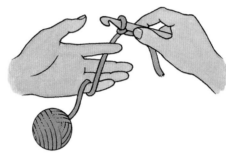

3 To control the supply and keep an even gauge on the yarn, hold the short end of the yarn in place with your right thumb. Take the yarn coming from the ball loosely around the little finger of your left hand and loop it over the left forefinger. Use the middle finger on the same hand to help hold the work. If you are left-handed, hold the hook in the left hand and the yarn in the right.

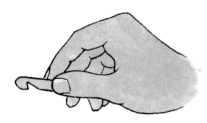

2 An alternative way to hold the hook is to grasp the flat section of the hook between your right thumb and forefinger as if you were holding a knife.

Making a slip knot

1 Loop the yarn as shown, insert the hook into the loop, catch the yarn with the hook, and pull it through to make a loop over the hook.

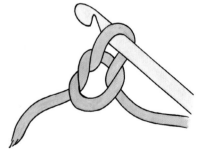

2 Gently pull the yarn to tighten the loop around the hook and complete the slip knot.

Working a foundation chain (ch)

The foundation chain is the equivalent of casting on in knitting and it's important to make sure that you have made the required number of chains for the pattern you are going to work. Count each V-shaped loop on the front of the chain as one chain stitch, except for the loop on the hook, which is not counted. You may find it easier to turn the chain over and count the stitches on the back of the chain. When working the first row of stitches (usually called the foundation row) into the chain, insert the hook under one thread or two, depending on your preference.

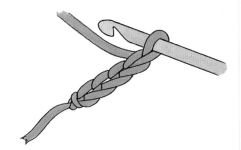

1 Holding the hook with the slip knot in your right hand and the yarn in your left, wrap the yarn over the hook. Draw the yarn through to make a new loop and complete the first chain stitch.

2 Repeat this step, drawing a new loop of yarn through the loop already on the hook until the chain is the required length. Move the thumb and second finger that are grasping the chain upward after every few stitches to keep the gauge even. When working into the chain, insert the hook under one thread (for a looser edge) or two (for a firmer edge), depending on your preference.

Working a single crochet (sc)

1 Begin with a foundation chain (see left) and insert the hook from front to back into the second chain from the hook. Wrap the yarn over the hook (yarn over) and draw it through the first loop, leaving two loops on the hook.

2 To complete the stitch, yarn over and draw it through both loops on the hook, leaving one loop on the hook. Continue in this way, working one single crochet into each chain.

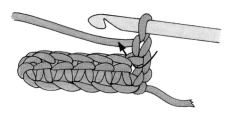

3 At the end of the row, turn and work one chain for the turning chain (remember that this chain does not count as a stitch). Insert the hook into the first single crochet at the beginning of the row. Work a single crochet into each stitch of the previous row, being careful to work the final stitch into the last stitch of the row, but not into the turning chain.

Working a slip stitch (sl st)

Slip stitch is the shortest of all the crochet stitches and its main uses are for joining rounds, making seams, and carrying the hook and yarn from one place to another. Insert the hook from front to back into the required stitch. Wrap the yarn over the hook (yarn over) and draw it through both the work and the loop on the hook. One loop remains on the hook and one slip stitch has been worked.

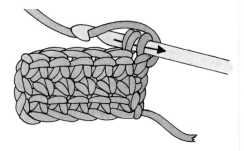

Working a half double crochet (hdc)

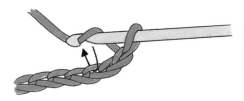

1 Begin with a foundation chain (see page 13), wrap the yarn over the hook (yarn over), and insert the hook into the third chain from the hook.

2 Draw the yarn through the chain, leaving three loops on the hook. Yarn over and draw through all three loops on the hook, leaving one loop on the hook. One half double crochet complete.

3 Continue along the row, working one half double crochet into each chain. At the end of the row, work two chains to turn. Skip the first stitch and work a half double crochet into each stitch made on the previous row. At the end of the row, work the last stitch into the top of the turning chain.

Working a double crochet (dc)

1 Begin with a foundation chain (see page 13), wrap the yarn over the hook, and insert the hook into the fourth chain from the hook.

2 Draw the yarn through the chain, leaving three loops on the hook. Yarn over again and draw the yarn through the first two loops on the hook, leaving two loops on the hook.

3 Yarn over and draw the yarn through the two loops on the hook leaving one loop on the hook. One double crochet complete. Continue along the row, working one double crochet stitch into each chain. At the end of the row, work three chains to turn. Skip the first stitch and work a double crochet into each stitch made on the previous row. At the end of the row, work the last stitch into the top of the turning chain.

Working a treble crochet (tr)

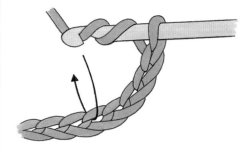

1 Begin with a foundation chain (see page 13), wrap the yarn over the hook twice (yarn over twice), and insert the hook into the fifth chain from the hook.

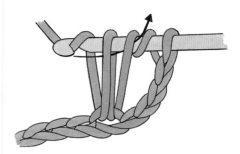

2 Draw the yarn through the chain, leaving four loops on the hook. Yarn over again and draw the yarn through the first two loops on the hook, leaving three loops on the hook.

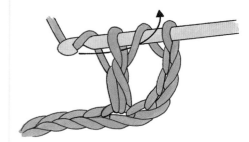

3 Yarn over again and draw through the first two loops on the hook leaving two loops on the hook.

4 Yarn over again and draw through the two remaining loops, leaving one loop on the hook. Treble crochet is now complete.

5 Continue along the row, working one treble crochet stitch into each chain. At the end of the row, work four chains to turn. Skip the first stitch and work a treble crochet into each stitch made on the previous row. At the end of the row, work the last stitch into the top of the turning chain.

Working a double treble crochet

A double treble stitch is similar to a treble. To make this stitch, follow the treble instructions, but at step 1, wrap the yarn over the hook three times. Work step 2, and then work step 3 twice, before proceeding to step 4.

Working in rounds

Most flowers are worked in rounds, which means that they are worked outward from a central ring called a foundation ring.

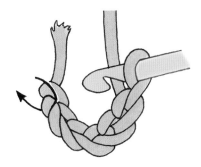

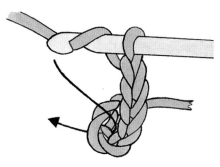

Making a foundation ring
Work a short length of foundation chain (see page 13) as specified in the pattern. Join the chains into a ring by working a slip stitch into the first stitch of the foundation chain.

Working into the ring
1 Work the number of turning chains specified in the pattern—three chains are shown here (counting as a double crochet stitch). Inserting the hook into the space at the center of the ring each time, work the number of stitches specified in the pattern into the ring. Count the stitches at the end of the round to check you have worked the correct number.

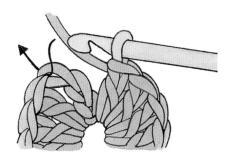

2 Join the first and last stitches of the round together by working a slip stitch into the top of the turning chain.

Finishing off the final round

To make a neat edge, finish off the final round by using this method of sewing the first and last stitches together in preference to the slip-stitch joining method shown on page 18.

1 Cut the yarn, leaving an end of about 4 in (10 cm) and draw it through the last stitch. With right side facing, thread the end in a large tapestry needle and take it under both loops of the stitch next to the turning chain.

2 Pull the needle through and insert it into the center of the last stitch of the round. On the wrong side, pull the needle through to complete the stitch, adjust the length of the stitch to close the round, then weave in the end on the wrong side in the usual way.

Working into the front and back

Unless pattern details instruct you otherwise, it's usual to work crochet stitches under both loops of the stitches made on the previous row.

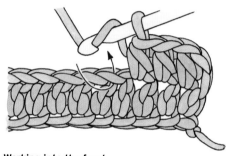

Working into the front
When instructions tell you to work into the front of the stitches, insert the hook only under the front loops of stitches on the previous row.

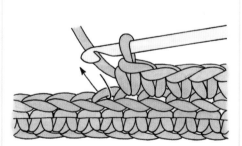

Working into the back
Likewise, to work into the back of the stitches, insert the hook only under the back loops of stitches on the previous row.

Changing colors

Some of the motifs in this book use more than one color. Changing the color of your yarn is simple to do.

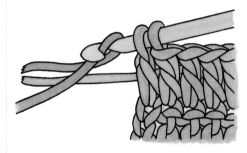

1 To make a neat join between colors, leave the last stitch of the old color incomplete so there are two loops on the hook and wrap the new color around the hook.

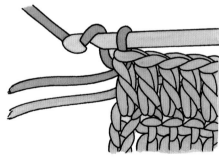

2 Draw the new color through to complete the stitch and continue working in the new color. The illustrations show a color change in a row of double crochet stitches–the method is the same for single crochet and other stitches.

Blocking and Joining

Whether your motifs will be used individually as appliques or ornaments, or joined to produce a larger piece, careful finishing will yield a beautiful project. Blocking your motifs ensures their even geometry, which will both improve their appearance and make them easier to join. When joining motifs, your choice of seam can produce a variety of effects, from barely visible joints to ones that add their own texture and interest to the finished piece. Don't be afraid to experiment with both blocking setups and joining methods, until you find the ones that work best for you.

Blocking

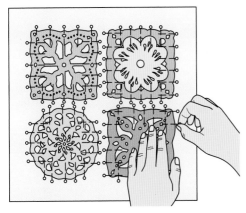

Some motif designs tend to curl or twist, after crocheting, and few will have perfect, consistent geometry every time they're made. Blocking your finished pieces will improve their flatness, neatness, and geometry, and help them hold their shape.

1 Make a blocking board. Secure a sheet of cotton fabric to a flat piece of cork board, Styrofoam, or other pin-friendly material. (You may also use an old quilt, pillow, or ironing board as a blocking board.)

2 Soak your motif with cold water. (For applications where stiffness is desirable, such as hanging ornaments, use laundry starch or fabric stiffener instead of water.) Gently squeeze out the excess liquid, and press the motif approximately to shape.

3 Lay the motif on the blocking board, and gently stretch the sides into shape until the piece is flat and even, and its dimensions are correct.

4 Secure the motif to the board with rustproof straight pins. Let it dry completely before removing it.

Joining finished blocks

Finished blocks can be joined together either by sewing or by crocheting them together with a hook. Always block the pieces before joining and use the same yarn for joining as you used for working the blocks. Begin by laying out the blocks in the correct order with the right or wrong side of each one facing upward, depending on the joining method you have chosen. Working first in horizontal rows, join the blocks together, beginning with the top row. Repeat until all the horizontal edges are joined. Turn the work so the remaining edges of the blocks are now horizontal and, as before, join these edges together.

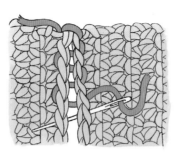

Working a woven seam
Lay the blocks out with the edges touching and wrong sides facing upward. Using matching yarn threaded in a tapestry needle, weave around the centers of the stitches as shown, without pulling the stitches too tightly. Work in the same way when joining row ends.

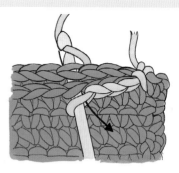

Working a slip-stitch seam
Joining blocks with wrong sides together gives a firm seam with an attractive ridge on the right side. If you prefer the ridge not to be visible, join the blocks with right sides together so the ridge is on the wrong side. Work a row of slip stitch (see page 13) through both loops of each block. When working this method along side edges of blocks worked in rows, work enough evenly spaced stitches so the seam is not too tight.

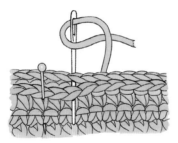

Working a back stitch seam
Hold the blocks to be joined with right sides together, pinning if necessary. Using matching yarn threaded in a tapestry needle, work a back stitch seam along the edge.

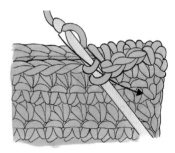

Working a single crochet seam
Work as for the slip stitch seam above, but work rows of single crochet stitches from the right or wrong side, depending on your preference.

Joining as you go

Blocks worked in rounds may also be joined in the outside round, so that each block is added to the finished project as it is crocheted. Blocks with picots and chains on the edges are most easily joined this way.

Joining with picots

1 Work the first block as given in the instructions.

2 Then work the second block as far as the first picot to be joined, and work to the central chain of the picot—for example, on a 5-ch picot, work 2 ch.

3 With the right side of first block facing up, insert the hook from below, through the center of the corresponding picot, and work a slip stitch, which counts as 1 chain (see diagram, below).

4 Complete the picot, then continue the final round of the second block to the next picot to be joined.

5 Repeat steps 3 and 4 as required, then complete the final round of the second block, and fasten off. Where several blocks meet together, insert the hook into the picot diagonally opposite.

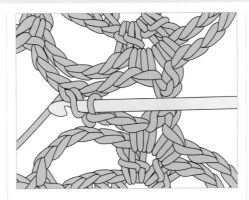

Joining with chains

Blocks with chained trim around the edges may be joined in a similar manner to those with picots. When making the second block, instead of working each joining slip stitch into a picot, work it into the middle stitch of the first block's corresponding chain. (If a chain is an even number of stitches long, join two stitches in the middle, instead of one.)

Solid joint

This joining method may be used to join new blocks as you go, regardless of the stitch types used in the outer edge (chains or picots are not required).

1 Work the first block according to the instructions.

2 Then work the second block as far as the side to be joined.

3 Begin the first stitch of the joining side as you normally would, until you come to the last yarn over of the stitch. Then hold the first block next to the second, with the right side facing, and align the blocks so that the stitch you're making is next to a corresponding stitch in the first block.

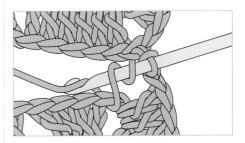

4 Instead of wrapping the yarn around the hook for the final yarn over, draw a loop through the back strand only of the nearest stitch of the first block, and through all loops of yarn on the hook, completing the stitch.

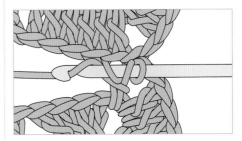

5 Repeat steps 3 and 4 for each stitch of the side.

2 Motif Collection

The motif collection begins by displaying the 75 beautiful designs that feature in this book. Flip through this colorful visual guide, select your design, and then turn to the relevant page of instructions to create your chosen piece. The instructions feature a chart, finished photograph, and written instructions. This is so that you can use either method or, better still, combine both.

Squares

Lace-crossed Square
Page 41

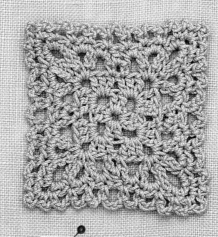

Ruffle-edged Square
Page 62

Dahlia Square
Page 66

Branched Square
Page 64

Leafy Square
Page 85

Rippling Square
Page 67

Floating-flower Square
Page 90

Gossamer Square
Page 65

Framed Square
Page 40

Daisy-centered Square
Page 63

Medallions

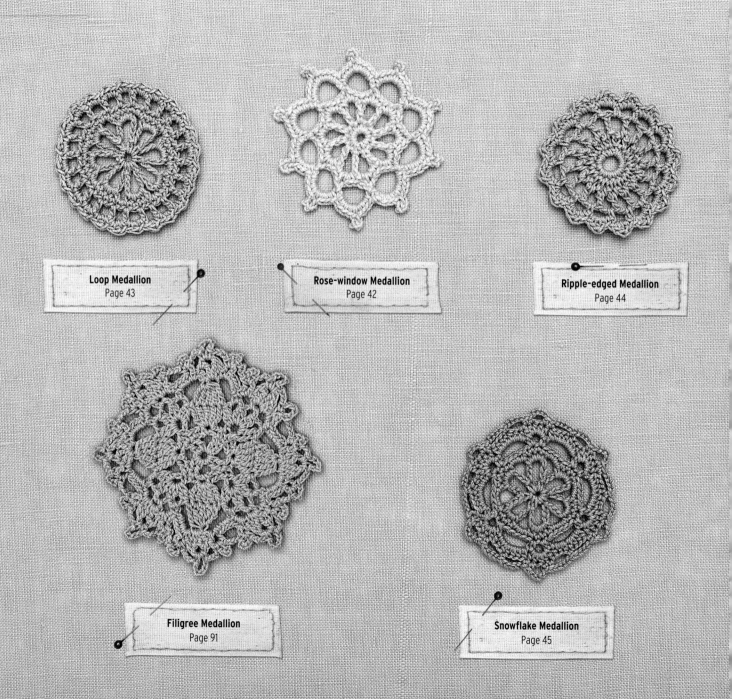

Loop Medallion
Page 43

Rose-window Medallion
Page 42

Ripple-edged Medallion
Page 44

Filigree Medallion
Page 91

Snowflake Medallion
Page 45

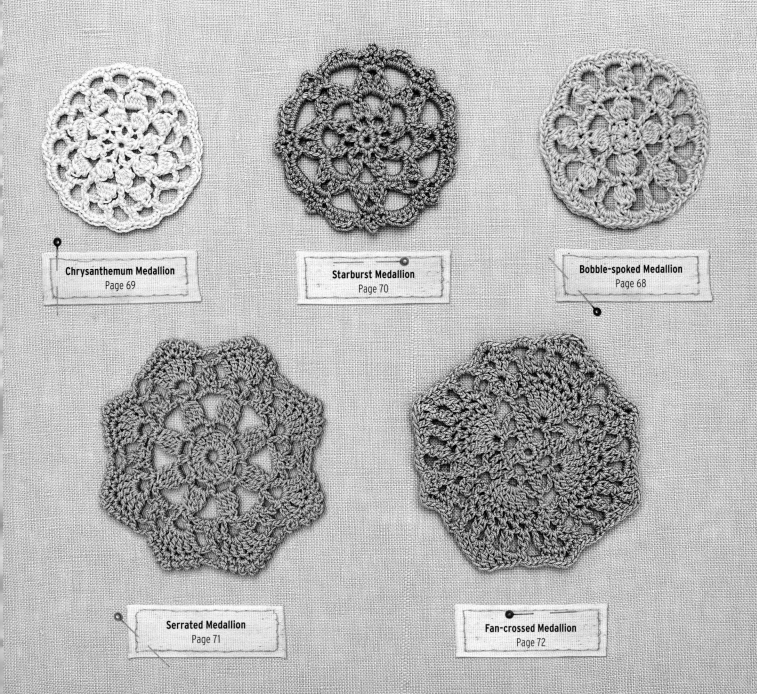

Chrysanthemum Medallion
Page 69

Starburst Medallion
Page 70

Bobble-spoked Medallion
Page 68

Serrated Medallion
Page 71

Fan-crossed Medallion
Page 72

Hexagons

Curve-lined Hexagon
Page 73

Swirled Hexagon
Page 76

Offset-snowflake Hexagon
Page 97

Hurricane Hexagon
Page 49

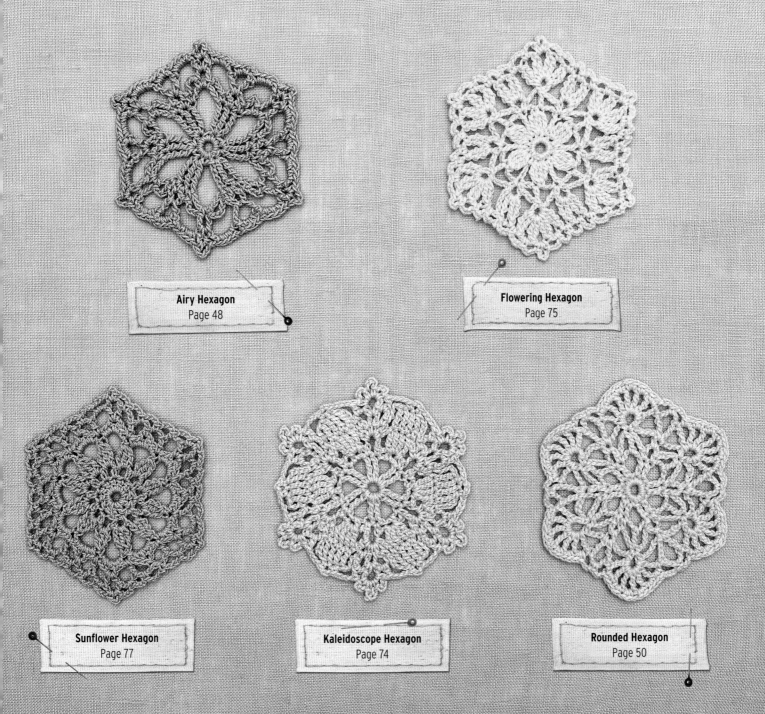

Airy Hexagon
Page 48

Flowering Hexagon
Page 75

Sunflower Hexagon
Page 77

Kaleidoscope Hexagon
Page 74

Rounded Hexagon
Page 50

Wildlife

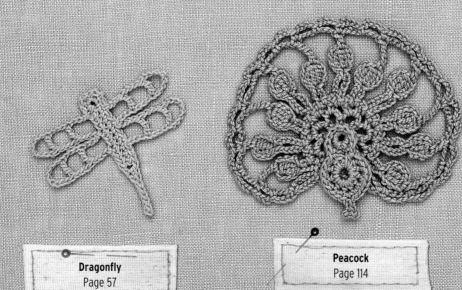

Hummingbird
Page 113

Butterfly
Page 115

Dragonfly
Page 57

Peacock
Page 114

Songbird
Page 112

Sealife

Seahorse
Page 60

Angel Fish
Page 111

Starfish
Page 61

Sand Dollar
Page 81

Scallop Shell
Page 80

Flowers

Chrysanthemum
Page 52

Flower with Stem
Page 55

Garden Hexagon
Page 96

Water Lily
Page 98

Sunflower
Page 53

Spiral Flower
Page 54

Branch
Page 78

Rounded Blossom
Page 51

Fruit & Vegetables

Pear
Page 59

Pumpkin
Page 102

Apple
Page 58

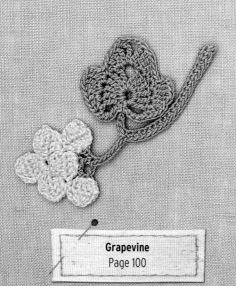

Grapevine
Page 100

Apple Basket
Page 101

Lemon Tree
Page 99

Sun, Moon & Stars

Star of David
Page 56

Sun
Page 82

Moon
Page 83

Star-crossed Star
Page 84

Lace Star
Page 56

Six-pointed Star
Page 51

Snowflakes

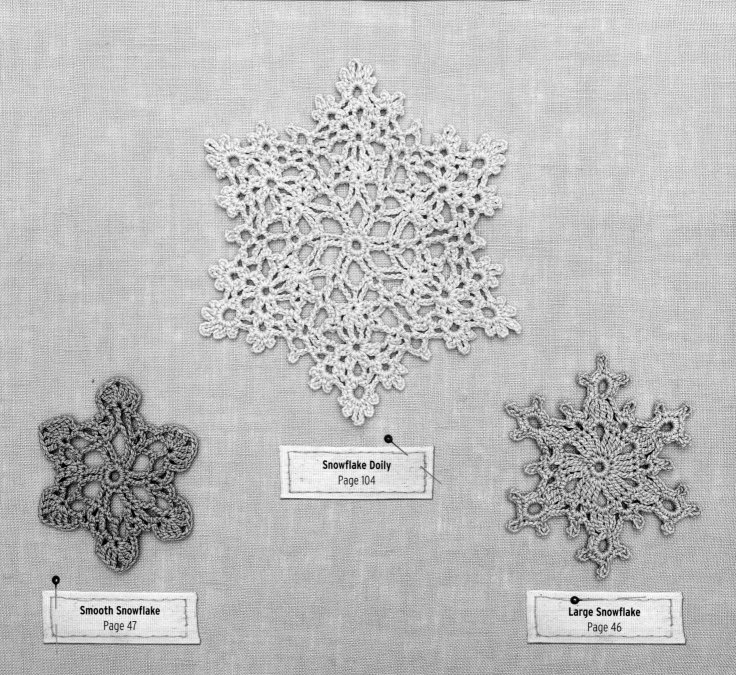

Snowflake Doily
Page 104

Smooth Snowflake
Page 47

Large Snowflake
Page 46

Special Occasions

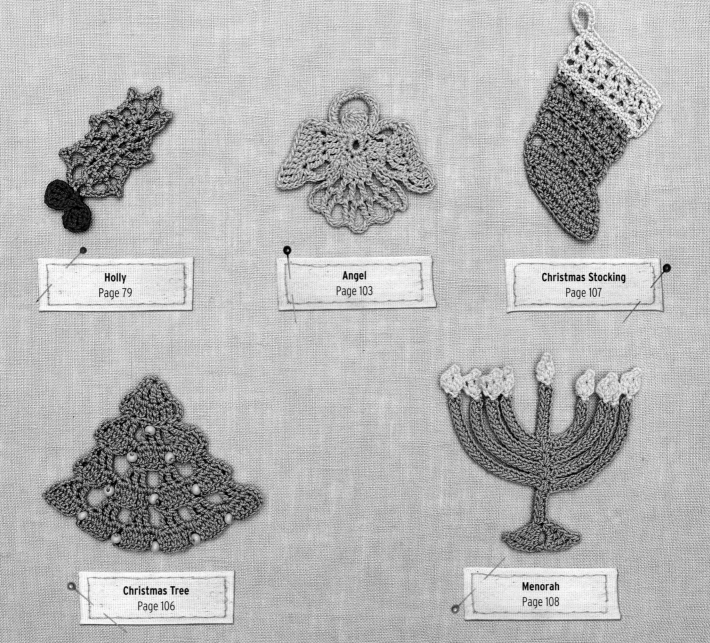

Holly
Page 79

Angel
Page 103

Christmas Stocking
Page 107

Christmas Tree
Page 106

Menorah
Page 108

Hearts

Floral Heart
Page 88

Ruffled Heart
Page 87

Tiny Heart
Page 52

Lace Heart
Page 86

Hobbies

Kite
Page 110

Hot Air Balloon
Page 109

Doilies

Scallop-edged Doily
Page 94

Vortex Doily
Page 92

1 Framed Square

Finished width: 2 in (51 mm)

Thread required: 8 yds (7.3 m)

Foundation ring: ch 5, and join with sl st in first ch.
Rnd 1: ch 1 (counts as sc). 7 sc in ring. Join with sl st in initial ch 1.
Rnd 2: ch 4 (counts as tr). 5 tr in same ch as last sl st. *ch 2. Skip 1 sc.** 6 tr in 1 sc. Repeat from * twice, and from * to ** once more. Join with sl st in top of initial ch 4.
Rnd 3: sl st in 2 tr, and ch 3 (counts as dc). dc in 1 tr. *[4 tr, ch 3, 4 tr] in next ch 2 space.** Skip 2 tr, and dc in 2 tr. Repeat from * twice, and from * to ** once more. Join with sl st in top of initial ch 3.
Rnd 4: ch 2 (counts as hdc). hdc in 1 dc. *ch 6. [2 hdc, ch 4, 2 hdc] in next ch 3 point. ch 6.** Skip 4 tr, and hdc in 2 dc. Repeat from * twice, and from * to ** once more. Join with sl st in top of initial ch 2.
Rnd 5: ch 1 (counts as sc). sc in hdc. *ch 7. Skip ch 6 space, and skip 2 hdc. [2 sc, ch 3, 2 sc] in ch 4 point (at corner). ch 7.** Skip 2 hdc, and skip ch 6 space. sc in 2 hdc. Repeat from * twice, and from * to ** once more. Join with sl st in initial ch 1. Fasten off; weave in ends.

○ = ch   • = sl st   + = sc   ⊢——⊣ = hdc   ⊢—/—⊣ = dc   ⊢—//—⊣ = tr

2 Lace-crossed Square

Finished width: 2 in (51 mm)

Thread required: 8 yds (7.3 m)

Foundation ring: ch 5, and join with sl st in first ch.
Rnd 1: ch 3 (counts as dc). 2 dc in ring. *ch 3. 3 dc in ring.
Repeat from * twice. ch 3, and join with sl st in top of initial ch 3.
Rnd 2: sl st in 2 dc, and in ch 3 space. ch 3 (counts as dc), and dc in
same ch 3 space. *ch 7, and sl st in 7th ch from hook to form loop.
2 dc in same ch 3 space. ch 6 and sl st in 5th ch from hook. ch 1.**
2 dc in next ch 3 space. Repeat from * twice, and from * to ** once
more. Join with sl st in top of initial ch 3.
Rnd 3: sl st in dc, and in the next ch 7 loop. ch 3 (counts as dc). [3 dc,
ch 3, 4 dc] in the same loop. *[dc, ch 2, dc, ch 2, dc] in the next ch 5
loop.** [4 dc, ch 3, 4 dc] in the next ch 7 loop. Repeat from * twice,
and from * to ** once more. Join with sl st in top of initial ch 3.
Rnd 4: ch 3 (counts as dc). dc in 3 dc. *[2 dc, ch 3, 2 dc] in ch 3
space. dc in 4 dc. [ch 2, sc] in each of the next 2 ch 2 spaces,
skipping the dc between them. ch 2.** Skip 1 dc, and dc in 4 dc.
Repeat from * twice, and from * to ** once more. Join with sl st
in top of initial ch 3. Fasten off; weave in ends.

○ = ch   • = sl st   + = sc   ┝─── = dc

3 Rose-window Medallion

Finished diameter: 2⅝ in (67 mm)

Thread required: 7 yds (6.4 m)

Foundation ring: ch 5, and join with sl st in first ch.

Rnd 1: ch 1 (counts as sc). 9 sc in ring. Join with sl st in initial ch 1.

Rnd 2: ch 3 (counts as dc). [ch 3, dc] in each of next 9 sc. ch 3, and join with sl st in top of initial ch 3.

Rnd 3: sl st in next ch 3 space, and ch 1 (counts as sc). [sc, ch 2, 2 sc] in the same space. [2 sc, ch 2, 2 sc] in each of the next 9 ch 3 spaces. Join with sl st in initial ch 1.

Rnd 4: sl st in sc, and in ch 2 point. [ch 7, sl st] in each of the 9 remaining ch 2 points. ch 7, and join with sl st in sl st.

Rnd 5: sl st in ch 7 space, and ch 1 (counts as sc). 3 sc in same space. *ch 5, and sl st in 5th ch from hook to form picot. 4 sc in same ch 7 space.** 4 sc in next ch 7 space. Repeat from * 8 times, and from * to ** once more. Join with sl st in initial ch 1. Fasten off; weave in ends.

○ = ch • = sl st + = sc ⊢⟋⊣ = dc

4 Loop Medallion

Finished diameter: 2⅛ in (54 mm)

Thread required: 8 yds (7.3 m)

Foundation ring: ch 5, and join with sl st in first ch.
Rnd 1: ch 1 (counts as sc). [ch 8, sc] 7 times in ring. ch 8, and join with sl st in initial ch 1.
Rnd 2: sl st in 3 ch, and in ch 8 loop. ch 1 (counts as sc). 3 sc in same loop. *ch 2. 4 sc in next ch 8 loop. Repeat from * 6 times. ch 2, and join with sl st in initial ch 1.
Rnd 3: ch 1 (counts as sc). sc in 3 sc. *2 sc in ch 2 space.** sc in 4 sc. Repeat from * 6 times, and from * to ** once more. Join with sl st in initial ch 1.
Rnd 4: ch 2 (counts as hdc). *ch 2. Skip 1 sc, and hdc in 1 sc. Repeat from * 22 times. ch 2, and join with sl st in top of intial ch 2.
Rnd 5: sl st in ch 2 space, and ch 1 (counts as sc). [dc, sc] in same space. [sc, dc, sc] in each of the 23 remaining ch 2 spaces. Join with sl st in initial ch 1. Fasten off; weave in ends.

○ = ch ・ = sl st ⊹ = sc ⊢—— = hdc ⊢⁄—— = dc

5 Ripple-edged Medallion

Finished diameter: 2 in (51 mm)

Thread required: 7 yds (6.4 m)

Foundation ring: ch 8, and join with sl st in first ch.
Rnd 1: ch 1 (counts as sc). 15 sc in ring. Join with
sl st in initial ch 1.
Rnd 2: ch 1 (counts as sc). [ch 3, sc] in each of 15 sc.
ch 3, and join with sl st in intial ch 1.
Rnd 3: sl st in 1 ch, and in ch 3 space. ch 3 (counts
as dc). [ch 2, dc] in each of 15 ch 3 spaces. ch 2, and
join with sl st in top of initial ch 3.
Rnd 4: sl st in ch 2 space, and ch 1 (counts as sc).
[ch 3, sc] in each of the next 15 ch 2 spaces. ch 3,
and join with sl st in initial ch 1.
Rnd 5: sl st in ch 3 space, and ch 1 (counts as sc).
[hdc, dc, hdc, sc] in same ch 3 space. [sc, hdc, dc,
hdc, sc] in each of the 15 remaining ch 3 spaces. Join
with sl st in initial ch 1. Fasten off; weave in ends.

○ = ch   • = sl st   + = sc   ├── = hdc   ├─⟋─ = dc

6 Snowflake Medallion

Finished diameter: 2½ in (64 mm)

Thread required: 10 yds (9.1 m)

Foundation ring: ch 4, and join with sl st in first ch.

Rnd 1: ch 1 (counts as sc). [ch 8, sc] 5 times in ring. ch 8, and join with sl st in initial ch 1.

Rnd 2: sl st in 2 ch, and in ch 8 loop. ch 1 (counts as sc), and 3 sc in same loop. *ch 3. 4 sc in next ch 8 loop. Repeat from * 4 times. ch 3, and join with sl st in initial ch 1.

Rnd 3: ch 1 (counts as sc). sc in 3 sc. *3 sc in ch 3 space.** sc in 4 sc. Repeat from * 4 times, and from * to ** once more. Join with sl st in initial ch 1.

Rnd 4: sl st in 1 sc, and ch 1 (counts as sc). *ch 3. sc in next sc. ch 6.** Skip 5 sc, and sc in 1 sc. Repeat from * 4 times, and from * to ** once more. Join with sl st in initial ch 1.

Rnd 5: sl st in ch 3 loop, and ch 2 (counts as hdc). 4 hdc in same loop. *7 hdc in ch 6 space.** 5 hdc in next ch 3 loop. Repeat from * 4 times, and from * to ** once more. Join with sl st in top of initial ch 2.

Rnd 6: ch 1 (counts as sc), and sc in 1 hdc. *ch 4. Skip 1 hdc, and sc in 2 hdc. ch 4. Skip 3 hdc, and sc in 1 hdc. ch 4.** Skip 3 hdc, and sc in 2 hdc. Repeat from * 4 times, and from * to ** once more. Join with sl st in initial ch 1. Fasten off; weave in ends.

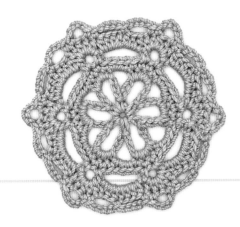

○ = ch • = sl st + = sc ├──┤ = hdc

7 Large Snowflake

Finished diameter: 3½ in (89 mm)

Thread required: 11 yds (10.1 m)

Foundation ring: ch 6, and join with sl st in first ch.

Rnd 1: ch 1 (counts as sc). 11 sc in ring. Join with sl st in initial ch 1.

Rnd 2: ch 4 (counts as tr). tr in same ch as last sl st. 2 tr in next sc. *ch 3. 2 tr in each of 2 sc. Repeat from * 4 times. ch 3, and join with sl st in top of initial ch 4.

Rnd 3: ch 1 (counts as sc). sc in 1 tr. *ch 3. sc in 2 tr. In ch 3 point: [sc, ch 3, tr, ch 8 and sl st in 8th ch from hook for loop, tr, ch 3, sc].** sc in 2 tr. Repeat from * 4 times, and from * to ** once more. Join with sl st in initial ch 1.

Rnd 4: sl st in sc, and in ch 3 loop. ch 1 (counts as sc). In same loop: [sc, ch 6 and sl st in 6th ch from hook for picot, 2 sc]. *ch 4. 3 sc in next ch 8 loop. In same loop, work: [ch 6 and sl st in 6th ch from hook for picot, 3 sc] 3 times. ch 4.** Skip: [sl st, tr, ch 3 space, 3 sc]. In next ch 3 loop (halfway between points) work: [2 sc, ch 6 and sl st in 6th ch from hook for picot, 2 sc]. Repeat from * 4 times, and from * to ** once more. Join with sl st in initial ch 1. Fasten off; weave in ends.

○ = ch   • = sl st   + = sc   ⊢—— = tr

8 Smooth Snowflake

Finished diameter: 2⅞ in (73 mm)

Thread required: 8 yds (7.3 m)

Foundation ring: ch 6 and join with sl st in first ch.

Rnd 1: ch 1 (counts as sc). 11 sc in ring. Join with sl st in initial ch 1.

Rnd 2: ch 4 (counts as tr). tr in 1 sc. *ch 6. tr in 2 sc. Repeat from * 4 times. ch 6, and join with sl st in top of initial ch 4.

Rnd 3: ch 1 (counts as sc). *ch 4, and sc in next tr. ch 6. tr in middle of ch 6 space. ch 6.** sc in tr. Repeat from * 4 times, and from * to ** once more. Join with sl st in initial ch 1.

Rnd 4: sl st in 1 ch, and in ch 4 loop. ch 1 (counts as sc). *ch 3, and sc in next ch 6 space. ch 3. [3 tr, ch 2, 3 tr] in tr. ch 3, and sc in next ch 6 space. ch 3.** sc in next ch 4 loop. Repeat from * 4 times, and from * to ** once more. Join with sl st in initial ch 1. Fasten off; weave in ends.

○ = ch   • = sl st   + = sc   ⊢——⊣ = tr

9 Airy Hexagon

Finished diameter: 3 in (76 mm)

Thread required: 10 yds (9.1 m)

Foundation ring: ch 6, and join with sl st in first ch.

Rnd 1: ch 1 (counts as sc). 11 sc in ring. Join with sl st in initial ch 1.

Rnd 2: ch 5 (counts as dtr). 2 dtr in same ch as last sl st. *ch 7. Skip 1 sc, and 3 dtr in 1 sc. Repeat from * 4 times. ch 7, and join with sl st in top of initial ch 5.

Rnd 3: ch 1 (counts as sc). *[dc, ch 2, dc] in 1 dtr. sc in 1 dtr. ch 4, and [sc, ch 5, sc] in middle of ch 7 space. ch 4.** sc in next dtr. Repeat from * 4 times, and from * to ** once more. Join with sl st in initial ch 1.

Rnd 4: sl st in dc, and in ch 2 space. ch 3 (counts as dc). ch 4, and dc in same ch 2 space. *ch 5. Skip dc, skip sc, and skip ch 4 space. [sc, ch 3, sc] in ch 5 loop. ch 5.** Skip ch 4 space, skip sc, and skip dc. [dc, ch 4, dc] in next ch 2 point. Repeat from * 4 times, and from * to ** once more. Join with sl st in top of initial ch 3.

Rnd 5: sl st in ch 4 space, and ch 1 (counts as sc). 2 sc in same ch 4 space. *ch 1, and 4 sc in ch 5 space. ch 1. [sc, ch 3, sc] in ch 3 loop. ch 1, and 4 sc in ch 5 space. ch 1.** 3 sc in ch 4 space. Repeat from * 4 times, and from * to ** once more. Join with sl st in initial ch 1. Fasten off; weave in ends.

10 Hurricane Hexagon

Finished diameter: 3 in (76 mm)

Thread required: 12 yds (11.0 m)

Foundation ring: ch 6, and join with sl st in first ch.

Rnd 1: ch 1 (counts as sc). 11 sc in ring. Join with sl st in initial ch 1.

Rnd 2: ch 5 (counts as dtr). [ch 2, dtr] in each of the next 11 sc. ch 2, and join with sl st in top of initial ch 5.

Rnd 3: ch 4 (counts as tr). dtr in same ch as last sl st. *ch 3. [tr, dtr] in next dtr. Repeat from * 10 times. ch 3, and join with sl st in top of initial ch 4.

Rnd 4: ch 1 (counts as sc). *sc in dtr. [sc, 2 hdc] in ch 3 space. 2 dc in tr. [4 tr, dc] in dtr. Skip ch 3 space.** sc in tr. Repeat from * 4 times, and from * to ** once more. Join with sl st in initial ch 1.

Rnd 5: ch 1 (counts as sc). *ch 4. Skip 3 stitches, and sc in hdc. ch 4. Skip 3 stitches, and sc in 1 tr. [ch 3, sc] in each of the next 3 stitches.** sc in 1 sc. Repeat from * 4 times, and from * to ** once more. Join with sl st in initial ch 1.

Rnd 6: ch 1 (counts as sc). *[ch 4, skip ch 4 space, and sc in sc] twice. [ch 3, skip ch 3 space, and sc in sc] twice. ch 3, skip ch 3 space, and skip 1 sc.** sc in 1 sc. Repeat from * 4 times, and from * to ** once more. Join with sl st in initial ch 1. Fasten off; weave in ends.

○ = ch   • = sl st   + = sc   ┠── = hdc   ┠─ = dc   ┠── = tr   ┠─── = dtr

11 Rounded Hexagon

Finished diameter: 3 in (76 mm)

Thread required: 10 yds (9.1 m)

Foundation ring: ch 6, and join with sl st in first ch.
Rnd 1: ch 1 (counts as sc). 11 sc in ring. Join with sl st in initial ch 1.
Rnd 2: ch 3 (counts as dc). dc in 1 sc. *ch 5. dc in 2 sc. Repeat from * 4 times. ch 5, and join with sl st in top of initial ch 3.
Rnd 3: ch 1 (counts as sc). *ch 4, and sc in next dc. ch 4, and tr in middle of ch 5 space. ch 4.** sc in 1 dc. Repeat from * 4 times, and from * to ** once more. Join with sl st in initial ch 1.
Rnd 4: sl st in 1 ch, and in ch 4 loop. ch 1 (counts as sc). *ch 5. [sc, ch 5, sc] in next tr. ch 5.** Skip ch 4 space, and sc in next ch 4 loop. Repeat from * 4 times, and from * to ** once more. Join with sl st in initial ch 1.
Rnd 5: ch 4 (counts as tr). ch 5, and tr in same ch as last sl st. *Skip ch 5 space, and skip sc. tr in the next ch 5 point. [ch 1, tr] 6 times in the same ch 5 point.** Skip sc, and skip ch 5 space. [tr, ch 5, tr] in next sc. Repeat from * 4 times, and from * to ** once more. Join with sl st in top of initial ch 4.
Rnd 6: sl st in 2 ch, and in ch 5 space. ch 1 (counts as sc). *ch 3. Skip 2 tr. 2 sc in each of 3 ch 1 spaces, skipping tr between. ch 1. 2 sc in each of next 3 ch 1 spaces. ch 3.** Skip 2 tr, and sc in middle of ch 5 space. Repeat from * 4 times, and from * to ** once more. Join with sl st in initial ch 1. Fasten off; weave in ends.

○ = ch   • = sl st   + = sc   ⊢— = dc   ⊢-— = tr

12 Rounded Blossom

Finished diameter: 1⅞ in (48 mm)

Thread required: 5 yds (4.6 m)

Foundation ring: ch 4, and join with sl st in first ch.
Rnd 1: ch 3 (counts as dc). 7 dc in ring. Join with sl st in top of initial ch 3.
Rnd 2: ch 1 (counts as sc). [ch 5, sc] in each of the next 7 dc. ch 5. Join with sl st in initial ch 1.
Rnd 3: *ch 4. [tr, dtr, ch 1, dtr, tr] in ch 5 loop. ch 4.** sl st in next sc. Repeat from * 6 times, and from * to ** once more. Join with sl st in sl st. Fasten off; weave in ends.

13 Six-pointed Star

Finished diameter: 2⅛ in (54 mm)

Thread required: 5 yds (4.6 m)

Foundation ring: ch 6, and join with sl st in first ch.
Rnd 1: ch 1 (counts as sc). 11 sc in ring. Join with sl st in initial ch 1.
Rnd 2: *ch 4, and tr in 1 sc. ch 4.** sl st in 1 sc. Repeat from * 4 times, and from * to ** once more. Join with sl st in sl st.
Rnd 3: *ch 3. dc in top of ch 4 space. [2 dc, tr, ch 5, tr, 2 dc] in tr. dc in ch 4 space. ch 3, and sl st in next sl st. Repeat from * 5 times. Fasten off; weave in ends.

○ = ch • = sl st + = sc ├── = hdc ├─├ = dc ├─⫻ = tr ├─⫻⫻ = dtr

14 Tiny Heart

Finished diameter: 1⅛ in (29 mm)

Thread required: 3 yds (2.7 m)

Foundation ring: ch 5, and join with sl st in first ch.
Rnd 1: ch 4. 7 tr in ring. ch 4, and sl st in 4th ch from hook to form loop. 7 tr in ring. ch 4, and sl st in ring.
Rnd 2: 4 sc in ch 4 space. hdc in 1 tr. 2 dc in each of 6 tr. [2 sc, ch 2, 2 sc] in ch 4 loop. 2 dc in each of 6 tr. hdc in tr, and 4 sc in ch 4 space. Join with sl st in sl st. Fasten off; weave in ends.

15 Chrysanthemum

Finished diameter: 1¾ in (44 mm)

Thread required: 5 yds (4.6 m)

Foundation ring: ch 5, and join with sl st in first ch.
Rnd 1: ch 1 (counts as sc). 7 sc in ring. Join with sl st in initial ch 1.
Rnd 2: ch 1 (counts as sc). [ch 3, sc] in each of 7 sc. ch 3, and join with sl st in initial ch 1.
Rnd 3: sl st in ch 3 space, and ch 1 (counts as sc). [ch 6, sc] in same space. *ch 1. [sc, ch 6, sc] in next ch 3 space. Repeat from * 6 times. ch 1, and join with sl st in initial ch 1.
Rnd 4: sl st in next ch 6 loop, and ch 1 (counts as sc). [4 sc, ch 2, 5 sc] in same ch 6 loop. *sl st in next ch 1 space (between loops).** [5 sc, ch 2, 5 sc] in next ch 6 loop. Repeat from * 6 times, and from * to ** once more. Join with sl st in initial ch 1. Fasten off; weave in ends.

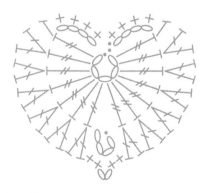

○ = ch • = sl st + = sc ├── = hdc ├─── = dc ├─⫣─ = tr

○ = ch • = sl st + = sc

16 Sunflower

Finished diameter: 2⅝ in (67 mm)

Thread required: color A, 4 yds (3.7 m); color B, 7 yds (6.4 m)

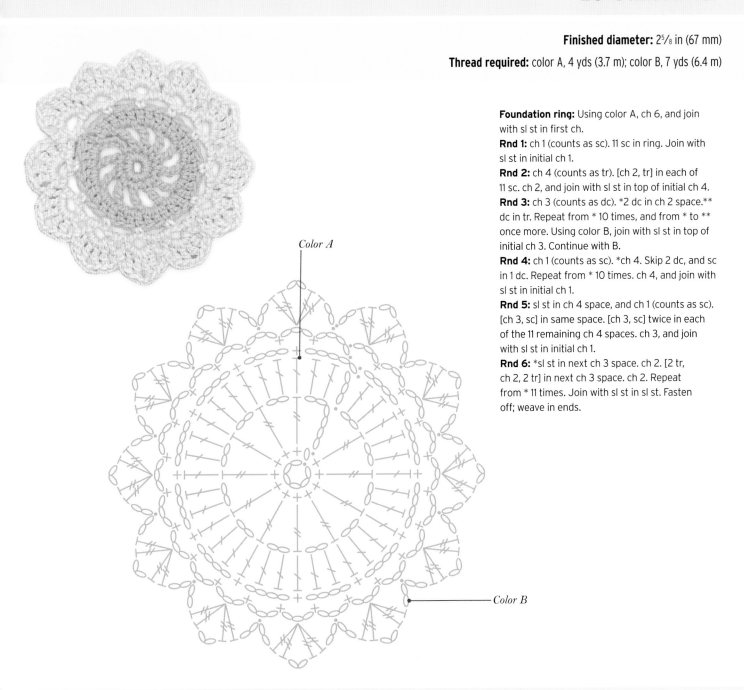

Color A

Color B

Foundation ring: Using color A, ch 6, and join with sl st in first ch.

Rnd 1: ch 1 (counts as sc). 11 sc in ring. Join with sl st in initial ch 1.

Rnd 2: ch 4 (counts as tr). [ch 2, tr] in each of 11 sc. ch 2, and join with sl st in top of initial ch 4.

Rnd 3: ch 3 (counts as dc). *2 dc in ch 2 space.** dc in tr. Repeat from * 10 times, and from * to ** once more. Using color B, join with sl st in top of initial ch 3. Continue with B.

Rnd 4: ch 1 (counts as sc). *ch 4. Skip 2 dc, and sc in 1 dc. Repeat from * 10 times. ch 4, and join with sl st in initial ch 1.

Rnd 5: sl st in ch 4 space, and ch 1 (counts as sc). [ch 3, sc] in same space. [ch 3, sc] twice in each of the 11 remaining ch 4 spaces. ch 3, and join with sl st in initial ch 1.

Rnd 6: *sl st in next ch 3 space. ch 2. [2 tr, ch 2, 2 tr] in next ch 3 space. ch 2. Repeat from * 11 times. Join with sl st in sl st. Fasten off; weave in ends.

○ = ch • = sl st + = sc ├─── = dc ├─#─ = tr

17 Spiral Flower

Finished diameter: 2³/₄ in (70 mm)

Thread required: 7 yds (6.4 m)

Foundation ring: ch 4, and join with sl st in first ch.

Rnd 1: ch 3 (counts as dc). 7 dc in ring. Join with sl st in 3rd ch of initial ch 3.

Rnd 2: *ch 14. sl st in 4th ch from hook to form picot. ch 2. Working back down petal, skip 2 ch, and tr in 2 ch. dtr in 2 ch, and tr in 2 ch. ch 1. Skip 1 ch, and sl st in 1 ch.** sl st in next dc. Repeat from * 6 times, and from * to ** once more. Join with sl st in sl st. Fasten off; weave in ends.

○ = ch • = sl st ┼ = sc ├─── = dc ├─╫─ = tr ├─╫╫─ = dtr

18 Flower with Stem

Finished height: 3 in (76 mm)

Thread required: color A, 1 yd (0.9 m); color B, 5 yds (4.6 m); color C, 2 yds (1.8 m)

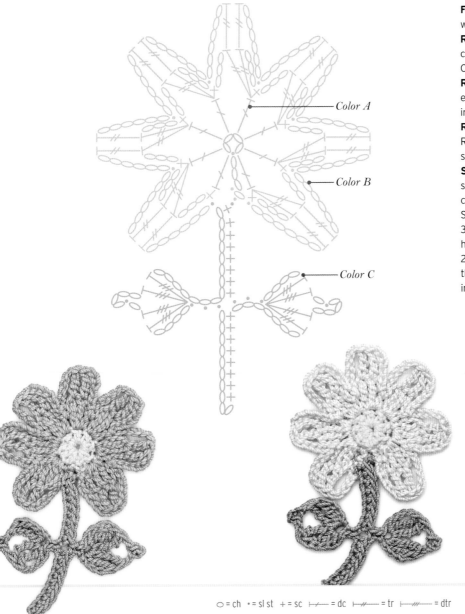

Color A

Color B

Color C

Foundation ring: Using color A, ch 4, and join with sl st in first ch.

Rnd 1: ch 3 (counts as dc). 8 dc in ring. Using color B, join with sl st in 3rd ch of initial ch 3. Continue with B.

Rnd 2: ch 1 (counts as sc). [sc, ch 3, 2 tr, ch 3] in each of the next 7 dc. sc in 1 sc. Join with sl st in initial ch 1.

Rnd 3: *sl st in next sc. ch 6. tr in next 2 tr. ch 6. Repeat from * 6 times. Using color C, join with sl st in sc. Continue with C.

Stem: ch 15. In 11th ch of ch 15: [2 dtr, ch 4 and sl st in 3rd ch from hook to form picot, ch 1, 2 dtr, ch 4, sl st]. sl st in 10th and 9th ch of ch 15. ch 10. Starting in 3rd ch from hook, sc in 8 ch. ch 7. In 3rd ch of ch 7: [2 dtr, ch 4 and sl st in 3rd ch from hook to form picot, ch 1, 2 dtr, ch 4, sl st]. sl st in 2nd and 1st ch of ch 7. sc in the 8 remaining ch of the ch 15. Join with sl st in sl st. Fasten off; weave in ends.

○ = ch   • = sl st   + = sc   ├─── = dc   ├──── = tr   ├───── = dtr

19 Star of David

Finished diameter: 2 in (51 mm)
Thread required: 5 yds (4.6 m)

20 Lace Star

Finished diameter: 2⅝ in (67 mm)
Thread required: 6 yds (5.5 m)

Foundation ring: ch 4, and join with sl st in first ch.
Rnd 1: ch 4 (counts as tr). [ch 3, tr] 5 times in ring. ch 3, and join with sl st in top of initial ch 4.
Rnd 2: ch 1 (counts as sc). [ch 2, sc] in same ch as last sl st. *3 sc in ch 3 space.** [sc, ch 2, sc] in tr. Repeat from * 4 times, and from * to ** once more. Join with sl st in initial ch 1.
Rnd 3: sl st in ch 2 point. *ch 10, and sl st in next ch 2 point. Repeat from * 4 times. ch 10, and join with sl st in sl st.
Rnd 4: *[4 sc, ch 3, 4 sc] in ch 10 space. sl st in sl st. Repeat from * 5 times. Fasten off; weave in ends.

21 Dragonfly

Finished height: 2 in (51 mm)

Thread required: 3 yds (2.7 m)

Foundation ring: ch 5, and join with sl st in first ch.

Rnd 1: ch 1 (counts as sc). 9 sc in ring. Join with sl st in initial ch 1.

Rnd 2: ch 4 (counts as tr). tr in 1 sc. *ch 6. tr in 2 sc. Repeat from * 3 times. ch 6, and join with sl st in top of initial ch 4.

Rnd 3: ch 1 (counts as sc). *ch 2. sc in next tr. ch 5. tr in ch 6 space. ch 5.** sc in tr. Repeat from * 3 times, and from * to ** once more. Join with sl st in initial ch 1.

Rnd 4: sl st in ch 2 point, and ch 1 (counts as sc). *ch 3, and sc in next ch 5 space. ch 3. In next tr, work: [dc, tr, ch 4 and sl st in 4th ch from hook for picot, tr, dc]. ch 3, and sc in next ch 5 space. ch 3.** sc in next ch 2 point. Repeat from * 3 times, and from * to ** once more. Join with sl st in initial ch 1. Fasten off; weave in ends.

Body: ch 12. Starting in 3rd ch from hook, sc in 9 ch. 5 sc in 1 ch (at end). Continuing down other side of chain, sc in 10 ch. ch 10. Starting in 3rd ch from hook, sl st in 5 ch, and sc in 2 ch. ch 1. Skip 1 ch of last ch 10, and skip ch 2 point. sl st in 3 sc.

Right Wings: *ch 16. tr in 9th ch from hook. ch 3. Continuing down chain, skip 3 ch, and tr in 1 ch. ch 3. Skip remaining 3 ch of wing, and skip 2 sc of body. sl st in 1 sc. Repeat from * once.

Head: *sl st in 1 sc, and 2 sc in 1 sc. Repeat from * once. sl st in 2 sc.

Left Wings: Repeat Right Wings. Fasten off; weave in ends.

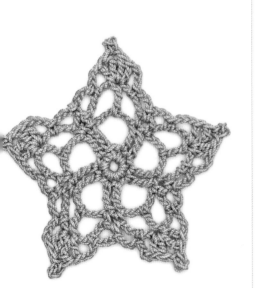

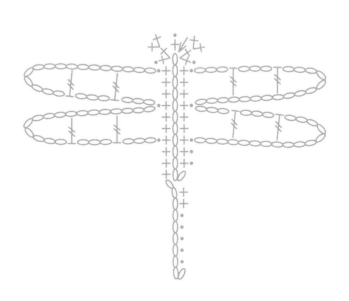

○ = ch · = sl st + = sc ⊢—— = tr ➤ = Beginning of dragonfly

22 Apple

Finished height: 2³/₈ in (60 mm)

Thread required: 8 yd (7.3 m)

Foundation ring: ch 6, and join with sl st in first ch.

Rnd 1: ch 5. 6 tr in ring. ch 3. 6 tr in ring. ch 5. sl st in ring.

Rnd 2: 5 sc in ch 5 space. hdc in 1 tr. dc in 5 tr. [2 dc, tr, ch 2, tr, 2 dc] in ch 3 space. dc in 5 tr. hdc in 1 tr. 5 sc in ch 5 space. Join with sl st in sl st.

Rnd 3: ch 3. Skip 3 sc, and 3 dc in each of the next 2 sc. tr in hdc, and in 4 dc. 3 dc in each of 2 dc. [tr, ch 2, dc] in 1 dc. hdc in tr, sl st in ch 2 space, and hdc in next tr. [dc, ch 2, tr] in 1 dc. 3 dc in each of 2 dc. tr in 4 dc, and in hdc. 3 dc in each of the next 2 sc. ch 3, skip 3 sc, and join with sl st in sl st.

Rnd 4: 3 sc in ch 3 space. sc in 2 dc. 2 sc in each of the next 6 stitches. sc in each of the next 10 stitches. [sc, ch 1, 3 sc] in ch 2 space. Skip dc, skip hdc, and sl st in sl st. Skip hdc and skip dc. [3 sc, ch 1, sc] in ch 2 space. sc in each of the next 10 stitches. 2 sc in each of the next 6 stitches. sc in 2 dc. 3 sc in ch 3 space. Join with sl st in sl st.

Stem: ch 11. In 6th ch of ch 11, work: [2 dtr, ch 3 and sl st in 3rd ch from hook to form picot, 2 dtr, ch 5, sl st]. sl st in next ch. ch 5. Beginning in 3rd ch from hook and working back down stem, sl st in 7 ch (work only in empty ch). Join with sl st in initial sc of Rnd 4. Fasten off; weave in ends.

23 Pear

Finished height: 2¾ in (70 mm)
Thread required: 8 yd (7.3 m)

Foundation ring: ch 6, and join with sl st in first ch.
Rnd 1: ch 5. 6 tr in ring. ch 3. 6 tr in ring. ch 5. sl st in ring.
Rnd 2: ch 2. 5 sc in ch 5 space. hdc in 1 tr. dc in 5 tr. [2 dc, tr, ch 4, tr, 2 dc] in ch 3 space. dc in 5 tr. hdc in 1 tr. 5 sc in ch 5 space. Join with sl st in top of initial ch 2.
Rnd 3: ch 3 (counts as dc). dc in 3 sc. 3 dc in 1 sc. dc in 3 stitches. 3 dc in 1 dc. dc in 4 dc. [dc, tr] in 1 dc. 3 tr in 1 tr. [3 tr, ch 1, 3 tr] in ch 4 point. 3 tr in 1 tr. [tr, dc] in 1 dc. dc in 4 dc. 3 dc in 1 dc. dc in 3 stitches. 3 dc in 1 sc. dc in 3 sc. Join with sl st in top of initial ch 3.
Rnd 4: ch 1 (counts as sc). sc in next 4 stitches. 2 sc in each of the next 8 stitches. sc in 12 stitches, and in ch 1 point. ch 9. In 4th ch of ch 9, work: [2 dtr, ch 3 and sl st in 3rd ch from hook to form picot, 2 dtr, ch 5, sl st]. sl st in 3rd ch of ch 9. ch 7. Starting in the 3rd ch from hook and working back down stem, sl st in 7 ch (work only in empty ch). sc in same ch 1 point as last sc. sc in 12 stitches, 2 sc in each of the next 8 stitches, and sc in 4 stitches. Join with sl st in initial ch 1. Fasten off; weave in ends.

○ = ch   • = sl st   + = sc   ⊢—₩—⊣ = tr   ⊢—₩₩—⊣ = dtr

24 Seahorse

Finished height: 2¼ in (57 mm)

Thread required: 3 yds (2.7 m)

Note: This pattern is crocheted in rounds around a foundation chain.

Foundation chain: ch 14.
Rnd 1: Starting in 3rd ch from hook, sc in 11 ch, and 5 sc in 1 ch (at end). Continuing around the other side of the chain, sc in 11 ch. Join with sl st in ch 2 point.
Rnd 2: ch 18. Starting in 3rd ch from hook, sl st in 3 ch. [ch 2, sl st] in 9 ch. [ch 3, skip 1 ch, and sc in 1 ch] twice. {Tail complete.} Returning to body, skip 1 ch, and sl st in 4 sc. [sl st, ch 5, dc] in 1 sc. [ch 3, dc] in 1 sc. ch 3. [dc, ch 5, sl st] in 1 sc. sl st in 7 sc. [ch 2, sl st] in 2 sc. ch 2. dc in 1 sc. ch 5. sc in 2nd ch of ch 5, and sl st in 1st ch of ch 5. [hdc, ch 1, sl st] in same sc as last dc. sl st in 3 sc. sc in 1 sc, hdc in 1 sc, and dc in 1 sc. 3 dc in 1 sc. dc in 1 sc, hdc in 1 sc, sc in 1 sc, and sl st in 1 sl st. Fasten off; weave in ends.

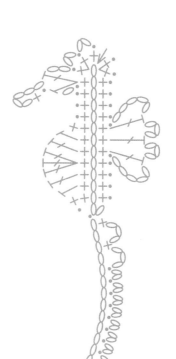

○ = ch   • = sl st   + = sc   ├── = hdc   ├──⟋ = dc   ⟶ = beginning of seahorse

25 Starfish

Finished diameter: 2½ in (64 mm)

Thread required: color A, 3 yds (2.7 m); color B, 4 yds (3.7 m)

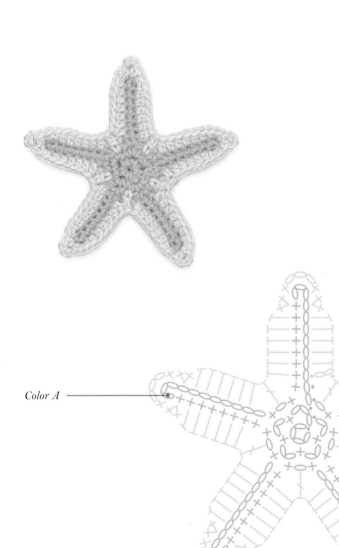

Color A

Color B

Foundation ring: Using color A, ch 4, and join with sl st in first ch.

Rnd 1: ch 1 (counts as sc). [ch 2, sc] 4 times in ring. ch 2, and join with sl st in initial ch 1.

Rnd 2: sl st in ch 2 point, and ch 1 (counts as sc). *ch 11. Starting in 4th ch from hook and working back down chain, sc in 8 ch. Back on ring, sc in same ch 2 point. ch 1.** sc in next ch 2 point. Repeat from * 3 times, and from * to ** once more. Join with sl st in initial ch 1.

Rnd 3: sl st in 1 ch. Using color B, sl st in 1 ch, and ch 2 (counts as hdc). Continue with B. hdc in 5 ch. *2 sc in 1 ch. [sc, ch 3, sc] in ch 3 point. 2 sc in 1 sc. hdc in 6 sc. Skip 2 sc, and dc in ch 1 space.** Skip sc, skip 1 ch, and hdc in 6 sc. Repeat from * 3 times, and from * to ** once more. Join with sl st in top of initial ch 2. Fasten off; weave in ends.

○ = ch • = sl st + = sc ┣── = hdc ┣─⟋ = dc

26 Ruffle-edged Square

Finished width: 2 in (51 mm)

Thread required: 9 yds (8.2 m)

Foundation ring: ch 5, and join with sl st in first ch.

Rnd 1: ch 3 (counts as dc). dc in ring. *ch 2. 2 dc in ring. Repeat from * twice. ch 2, and join with sl st in top of initial ch 3.

Rnd 2: sl st in dc, and in ch 2 space. ch 3 (counts as dc). [2 dc, ch 2, 3 dc] in same ch 2 space. [3 dc, ch 2, 3 dc] in each of the 3 remaining ch 2 spaces. Join with sl st in top of initial ch 3.

Rnd 3: ch 1 (counts as sc). *ch 4. [sc, ch 6, sc, ch 10, sc, ch 6, sc] in next ch 2 point. ch 4. Skip 2 dc, and sc in 1 dc. ch 2.** sc in next dc. Repeat from * twice, and from * to ** once more. Join with sl st in initial ch 1.

Rnd 4: sl st in ch 4 space, and ch 1 (counts as sc). sc in same space. *3 sc in next ch 6 loop. [2 sc, ch 3, 2 sc] in ch 10 loop. 3 sc in ch 6 loop. 2 sc in next ch 4 space, and dc in ch 2 space.** 2 sc in ch 4 space. Repeat from * twice, and from * to ** once more. Join with sl st in initial ch 1.

Rnd 5: ch 1 (counts as sc). *[ch 3, skip 1 sc, and sc in 1 sc] 3 times. ch 2. [sc, ch 3, sc] in ch 3 point. ch 2, and sc in 1 sc. [ch 3, skip 1 sc and sc in 1 sc] 3 times.** ch 4, skip dc, and sc in 1 sc. Repeat from * twice, and from * to ** once more. ch 4, and join with sl st in initial ch 1. Fasten off; weave in ends.

○ = ch • = sl st + = sc ⊢⟋⟍ = dc

27 Daisy-centered Square

Finished width: 2 in (51 mm)

Thread required: 8 yds (7.3 m)

Foundation ring: ch 6, and join with sl st in first ch.

Rnd 1: ch 4 (counts as tr). tr in ring. [ch 2, 2-tr decrease] 7 times in ring. ch 2. Skipping initial ch 4, join with sl st in top of 1st tr.

Rnd 2: ch 3 (counts as dc). ch 3, and dc in same stitch as last sl st. *4 dc in each of the next 2 ch 2 spaces.** [dc, ch 3, dc] in top of the next tr decrease. Repeat from * twice, and from * to ** once more. Join with sl st in top of initial ch 3.

Rnd 3: ch 3 (counts as dc). *ch 2. [dc, ch 3, dc] in ch 3 point. ch 2, and dc in 1 dc. [ch 2, skip 1 dc, and dc in 1 dc] twice. dc in 1 dc.** [ch 2, skip 1 dc, and dc in 1 dc] twice. Repeat from * twice, and from * to ** once more. ch 2, skip 1 dc, and dc in 1 dc. ch 2, and join with sl st in top of initial ch 3.

Rnd 4: sl st in ch 2 space. ch 2 (counts as hdc), and hdc in same space. *[3 hdc, ch 2, 3 hdc] in ch 3 point. 2 hdc in each of the next 3 ch 2 spaces. ch 1.** 2 hdc in each of the next 3 ch 3 spaces. Repeat from * twice, and from * to ** once more. 2 hdc in each of the next 2 ch 2 spaces. Join with sl st in top of initial ch 2. Fasten off; weave in ends.

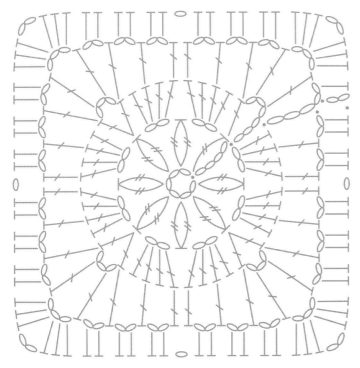

○ = ch   • = sl st   ├── = hdc   ├─/── = dc   ├─//── = tr

28 Branched Square

Finished width: 2 in (51 mm)

Thread required: 9 yds (8.2 m)

Foundation ring: ch 5, and join with sl st in first ch.

Rnd 1: ch 1 (counts as sc). sc in ring. *ch 3. [ch 6, and sl st in 6th ch from hook to form loop] 3 times. sl st in 3rd ch of last ch 3. ch 2, and sl st in top of last sc made.** 2 sc in ring. Repeat from * twice, and from * to ** once more. Join with sl st in initial ch 1.

Rnd 2: ch 4 (counts as tr). *ch 3. sc in next ch 6 loop. [ch 5, sc] in each of the next 2 ch 6 loops. ch 3.** tr in the next sc (at base of branch). Repeat from * twice, and from * to ** once more. Join with sl st in top of initial ch 4.

Rnd 3: sl st in ch 3 space, and ch 2 (counts as hdc). 2 hdc in same space. *4 hdc in next ch 5 space. [hdc, ch 2, hdc] in sc (at corner). 4 hdc in ch 5 space.** 3 hdc in each of the next 2 ch 3 spaces. Repeat from * twice, and from * to ** once more. 3 hdc in ch 3 space. Join with sl st in top of initial ch 2.

Rnd 4: sl st in 1 hdc, and ch 1 (counts as sc). sc in 6 hdc. *[sc, ch 4, sc] in ch 2 point. sc in 7 hdc. ch 2.** Skip 2 hdc, and sc in 7 hdc. Repeat from * twice, and from * to ** once more. Join with sl st in initial ch 1. Fasten off; weave in ends.

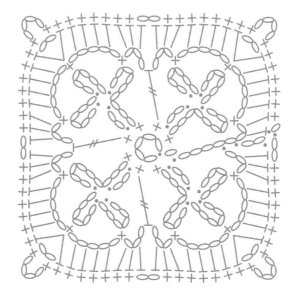

○ = ch •‒ = sl st + = sc ⊢‒ = hdc ⊢⊬ = tr

29 Gossamer Square

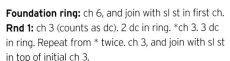

Finished width: 2 in (51 mm)

Thread required: 6 yds (5.5 m)

Foundation ring: ch 6, and join with sl st in first ch.

Rnd 1: ch 3 (counts as dc). 2 dc in ring. *ch 3. 3 dc in ring. Repeat from * twice. ch 3, and join with sl st in top of initial ch 3.

Rnd 2: ch 2 (counts as shortened dc). 2-dc decrease in next 2 dc. *ch 6. dc in ch 3 space. ch 6.** 3-dc decrease in next 3 dc. Repeat from * twice, and from * to ** once more. Join with sl st in top of initial decrease.

Rnd 3: ch 1 (counts as sc). *ch 4, and sc in ch 6 space. ch 3. In next dc, work: [tr, ch 4 and sl st in 4th ch from hook for picot, tr]. ch 3, and sc in next ch 6 space. ch 4.** sc in next dc decrease. Repeat from * twice, and from * to ** once more. Join with sl st in initial ch 1.

Rnd 4: sl st in 1 ch, and in ch 4 space. ch 2 (counts as hdc). *[ch 3, hdc] in next ch 3 space. ch 3. [2 hdc, ch 3, 2 hdc] in next ch 4 loop (at corner).** [ch 3, hdc] in next ch 3 space, and in each of 2 ch 4 spaces. Repeat from * twice, and from * to ** once more. [ch 3, hdc] in ch 3 space, and in ch 4 space. ch 3, and join with sl st in top of initial ch 2. Fasten off; weave in ends.

○ = ch • = sl st + = sc ⊢— = hdc ⊢—⁄ = dc ⊢—⁄⁄ = tr

30 Dahlia Square

Finished width: 2 in (51 mm)

Thread required: 9 yds (8.2 m)

Foundation ring: ch 5, and join with sl st in first ch.
Rnd 1: ch 3 (counts as dc). [ch 2, dc] 7 times in ring. ch 2, and join with sl st in top of initial ch 3.
Rnd 2: ch 3 (counts as dc). 4-dc cluster in same ch as last sl st. *ch 5. Make bobble (5-dc cluster) in next dc. Repeat from * 6 times. ch 5, and join with sl st in top of initial dc cluster.
Rnd 3: sl st in ch 5 space, and ch 1 (counts as sc). [2 sc, ch 2, 3 sc] in same ch 5 space. *ch 1. [3 sc, ch 2, 3 sc] in next ch 5 space. Repeat from * 6 times. ch 1, and join with sl st in initial ch 1.
Rnd 4: sl st in 2 sc, and in ch 2 point. ch 1 (counts as sc). *ch 4, and sc in next ch 1 space (halfway between points). ch 4, and sc in next ch 2 point. ch 4. In next ch 1 space: [tr, ch 6 and sl st in 5th ch from hook for picot, ch 1, tr].** ch 4, and sc in next ch 2 point. Repeat from * twice, and from * to ** once more. ch 4, and join with sl st in initial ch 1.
Rnd 5: sl st in next ch 4 space, and ch 1 (counts as sc). 3 sc in same space. 4 sc in each of the next 2 ch 4 spaces. *Skip ch 1 space. 5 sc in next ch 5 loop (at point). Skip ch 1 space.** 4 sc in each of the next 4 ch 4 spaces. Repeat from * twice, and from * to ** once more. 4 sc in ch 4 space. Join with sl st in initial ch 1. Fasten off; weave in ends.

○ = ch   • = sl st   + = sc   ⊢—⧸ = dc   ⊢—⧸⧸ = tr

33 Chrysanthemum Medallion

Finished diameter: 2³/₈ in (60 mm)
Thread required: 10 yds (9.1 m)

Foundation ring: ch 5, and join with sl st in first ch.
Rnd 1: ch 3 (counts as dc). [ch 2, dc] 7 times in ring. ch 2, and join with sl st in top of initial ch 3.
Rnd 2: ch 3 (counts as dc). 4-dc cluster in same ch as last sl st. *ch 5. Make bobble (5-dc cluster) in next dc. Repeat from * 6 times. ch 5, and join with sl st in top of initial dc cluster.
Rnd 3: ch 3 (counts as dc). *ch 5. 5-dc cluster in next ch 5 space.** ch 5, and dc in top of next bobble. Repeat from * 6 times, and from * to ** once more. ch 5, and join with sl st in top of initial ch 3.
Rnd 4: sl st in 2 ch, and in ch 5 space. ch 1 (counts as sc). [ch 5, sc] in each of the 15 remaining ch 5 spaces. ch 5, and join with sl st in initial ch 1.
Rnd 5: sl st in ch 5 space, and ch 1 (counts as sc). 4 sc in same ch 5 space. 5 sc in each of the 15 remaining ch 5 spaces. Join with sl st in initial ch 1. Fasten off; weave in ends.

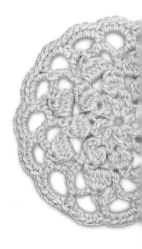

○ = ch   • = sl st   + = sc   ⊢—— = dc

34 Starburst Medallion

Finished diameter: 2³/₄ in (70 mm)
Thread required: 11 yds (10.1 m)

Foundation ring: ch 5, and join with sl st in first ch.
Rnd 1: ch 1 (counts as sc). 7 sc in ring. Join with sl st in initial ch 1.
Rnd 2: ch 1 (counts as sc). [ch 3, sc] in each of the 7 remaining sc. ch 3, and join with sl st in initial ch 1.
Rnd 3: sl st in ch 3 space, and ch 3 (counts as dc). 2-dc cluster in same ch 3 space. *ch 5. 3-dc cluster in next ch 3 space. Repeat from * 6 times. ch 5, and join with sl st in top of initial dc cluster.
Rnd 4: sl st in ch 5 space, and ch 1 (counts as sc). In same ch 5 space, work: [hdc, dc, tr, ch 2, tr, dc, hdc, sc]. In each of the 7 remaining ch 5 spaces, work: [sc, hdc, dc, tr, ch 2, tr, dc, hdc, sc]. Join with sl st in initial ch 1.
Rnd 5: sl st in hdc, in dc, in tr, and in ch 2 point. ch 1 (counts as sc). 3 sc in same ch 2 point. *ch 6. 4 sc in next ch 2 point. Repeat from * 6 times. ch 6, and join with sl st in initial ch 1.
Rnd 6: sl st in 1 sc, and ch 1 (counts as sc). *ch 4, and sc in next sc. ch 2. Skip 1 sc. In ch 6 space, work: [sc, hdc, 3 dc, hdc, sc]. ch 2.** Skip 1 sc, and sc in 1 sc. Repeat from * 6 times, and from * to ** once more. Join with sl st in initial ch 1. Fasten off; weave in ends.

○ = ch   ∙ = sl st   ✕ = sc   ⊢┬─ = hdc   ⊢┼─ = dc   ⊢╫─ = tr

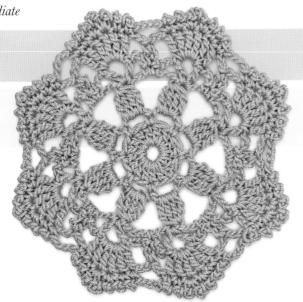

35 Serrated Medallion

Finished diameter: 3⅜ in (86 mm)

Thread required: 14 yds (12.8 m)

Foundation ring: ch 7, and join with sl st in first ch.

Rnd 1: ch 3 (counts as dc). 15 dc in ring. Join with sl st in top of initial ch 3.

Rnd 2: ch 1 (counts as sc). *ch 4. Skip 1 dc, and sc in 1 dc. Repeat from * 6 times. ch 4, and join with sl st in initial ch 1.

Rnd 3: sl st in next ch 4 space, and ch 4 (counts as tr). 3-tr cluster in same ch 4 space. *ch 7. 4-tr cluster in next ch 4 space. Repeat from * 6 times. ch 7, and join with sl st in top of initial cluster.

Rnd 4: ch 3 (counts as dc). ch 3, and dc in same cluster as last sl st. *ch 3. In the middle of the next ch 7 space work: [sc, ch 4 and sl st in 4th ch from hook to form loop, sc]. ch 3.** [dc, ch 3, dc] in top of next tr cluster. Repeat from * 6 times, and from * to ** once more. Join with sl st in top of initial ch 3.

Rnd 5: sl st in ch 3 point, and ch 4 (counts as tr). 5 tr in same ch 3 point. *ch 2. sc in next ch 4 loop (between tr groups). ch 2. Skip dc, and skip ch 3 space.** 6 tr in next ch 3 point. Repeat from * 6 times, and from * to ** once more. Join with sl st in top of initial ch 4.

Rnd 6: ch 1 (counts as sc). *[ch 2, sc] in 1 tr. ch 2. [sc, ch 2, sc] in 1 tr. ch 3. [sc, ch2, sc] in 1 tr. [ch 2, sc] in each of 2 tr. ch 4. Skip ch 2 space, skip sc, and skip next ch 2 space.** sc in next tr. Repeat from * 6 times, and from * to ** once more. Join with sl st in initial ch 1. Fasten off; weave in ends.

○ = ch   • = sl st   + = sc   ⊦—⊦ = dc   ⊦—⊦ = tr

36 Fan-crossed Medallion

Finished diameter: 3½ in (89 mm)

Thread required: 17 yds (15.5 m)

Foundation ring: ch 5, and join with sl st in first ch.

Rnd 1: ch 1 (counts as sc). 7 sc in ring. Join with sl st in initial ch 1.

Rnd 2: ch 3 (counts as dc). dc in 1 sc. *ch 3. dc in 2 sc. Repeat from * twice. ch 3, and join with sl st in top of initial ch 3.

Rnd 3: ch 3 (counts as dc). dc in 1 dc. *ch 4. [sc, ch 3, sc] in next ch 3 space. ch 4.** 2-dc decrease in next 2 dc. Repeat from * twice, and from * to ** once more. Skip initial ch 3, and join with sl st in initial dc.

Rnd 4: ch 3 (counts as dc). *ch 4. Skip ch 4 space, and 7 tr in ch 3 loop. ch 4.** Skip ch 4 space and dc in dc decrease. Repeat from * twice, and from * to ** once more. Join with sl st in top of initial ch 3.

Rnd 5: ch 3 (counts as dc). [dc, ch 2, 2 dc] in same ch as last sl st. *ch 3. Skip ch 4 space, and sc in next tr. [ch 2, sc] in each of next 6 tr. ch 3.** Skip ch 4 space, and [2 dc, ch 2, 2 dc] in dc. Repeat from * twice, and from * to ** once more. Join with sl st in top of initial ch 3.

Rnd 6: sl st in dc, and in ch 2 point. ch 3 (counts as dc). [dc, ch 2, 2 dc] in same ch 2 point. *ch 5. Skip 2 dc, skip ch 3 space, and skip sc. sc in ch 2 space. [ch 2, sc] in each of the next 5 ch 2 spaces. ch 5. Skip sc, skip ch 3 space, and skip 2 dc.** [2 dc, ch 2, 2 dc] in ch 2 space. Repeat from * twice, and from * to ** once more. Join with sl st in top of initial ch 3.

Rnd 7: ch 1 (counts as sc). *sc in next dc. [sc, ch 3, sc] in ch 2 space. sc in 2 dc. ch 5. Skip ch 5 space, and skip sc. 2-dc cluster in ch 2 space. [ch 4, and 2-dc cluster in next ch 2 space] 4 times. ch 5. Skip sc, and skip ch 5 space.** sc in dc. Repeat from * twice, and from * to ** once more. Join with sl st in initial ch 1.

Rnd 8: ch 1 (counts as sc). sc in 2 sc. *3 sc in ch 3 point. sc in 3 sc. 4 sc in ch 5 space. [sc, hdc, dc] in next ch 4 space. [dc, tr, dtr] in 1 ch 4 space. [dtr, tr, dc] in 1 ch 4 space. [dc, hdc, sc] in 1 ch 4 space. 4 sc in ch 5 space.** sc in 3 sc. Repeat from * twice, and from * to ** once more. Join with sl st in initial ch 1. Fasten off; weave in ends.

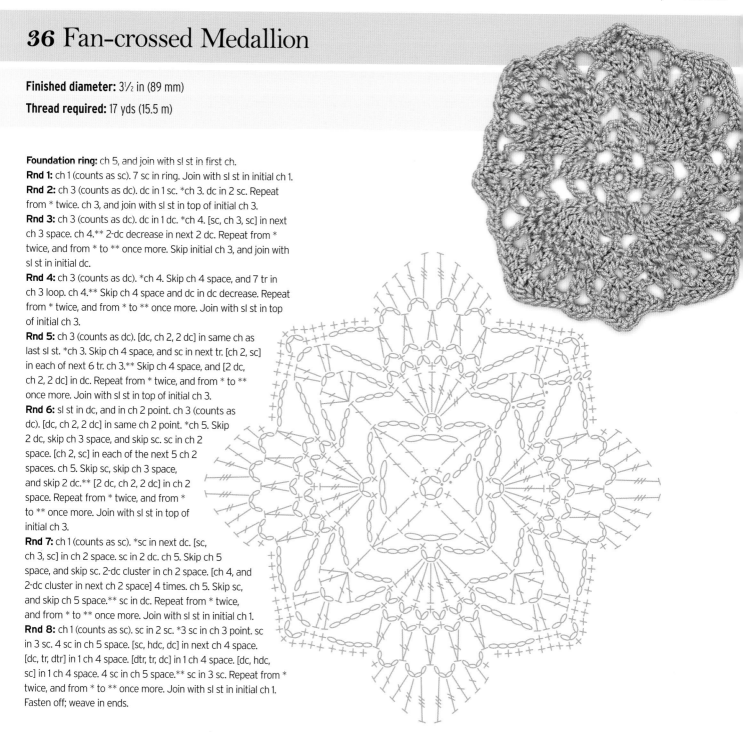

○ = ch   ·•· = sl st   + = sc   ├── = hdc   ├─ = dc   ├╫─ = tr   ├╫╫─ = dtr

37 Curve-lined Hexagon

Finished diameter: 3 in (76 mm)
Thread required: 13 yds (11.9 m)

Foundation ring: ch 6, and join with sl st in first ch.
Rnd 1: ch 4 (counts as tr). tr in ring. *ch 3. 2 tr in ring. Repeat from * 4 times. ch 3, and join with sl st in top of initial ch 4.
Rnd 2: ch 1 (counts as sc). *ch 5, and sc in next tr. ch 2, and sc in ch 3 space. ch 2.** sc in 1 tr. Repeat from * 4 times, and from * to ** once more. Join with sl st in initial ch 1.
Rnd 3: sl st in ch 5 loop, and ch 3 (counts as dc). [2 dc, ch 2, 3 dc] in same loop. *dc in each of the next 2 ch 2 spaces.** [3 dc, ch 2, 3 dc] in next ch 5 loop. Repeat from * 4 times, and from * to ** once more. Join with sl st in top of initial ch 3.
Rnd 4: ch 3 (counts as dc). dc in 2 dc. *[dc, ch 3, dc] in ch 2 point. dc in 3 dc. ch 2.** Skip 2 dc, and dc in 3 dc. Repeat from * 4 times, and from * to ** once more. Join with sl st in top of initial ch 3.
Rnd 5: sl st in 3 dc, and in ch 3 point. ch 1 (counts as sc). [ch 3, sc] in same ch 3 point. *ch 4. Skip 4 dc. [sc, ch 3, sc] in next ch 2 space. ch 4.** Skip 4 dc. [sc, ch 3, sc] in next ch 3 space. Repeat from * 4 times, and from * to ** once more. Join with sl st in initial ch 1.
Rnd 6: sl st in ch 3 point, and ch 2 (counts as hdc). [hdc, ch 2, 2 hdc] in same point. *4 hdc in ch 4 space, 3 hdc in ch 3 loop, and 4 hdc in ch 4 space.** [2 hdc, ch 2, 2 hdc] in ch 3 point. Repeat from * 4 times, and from * to ** once more. Join with sl st in top of initial ch 2. Fasten off; weave in ends.

○ = ch • = sl st + = sc ⊢—⁄ = dc ⊢— = hdc ⊢—⁄ = dc ⊢—⁄⁄ = tr

38 Kaleidoscope Hexagon

Finished diameter: 3 in (76 mm)

Thread required: 12 yds (11.0 m)

Foundation ring: ch 6, and join with sl st in first ch.
Rnd 1: ch 4 (counts as tr). tr in ring. *ch 3. 2 tr in ring. Repeat from * 4 times. ch 3, and join with sl st in top of initial ch 4.
Rnd 2: ch 1 (counts as sc). *ch 5, and sc in next tr. ch 2, and sc in ch 3 space. ch 2.** sc in 1 tr. Repeat from * 4 times, and from * to ** once more. Join with sl st in initial ch 1.
Rnd 3: sl st in 1 ch, and in ch 5 loop. ch 1 (counts as sc). In the same loop, work: [ch 3, sc, ch 5, sc, ch 3, sc]. *ch 2. Skip sc, skip ch 2 space. 4 tr in sc. ch 2.** Skip ch 2 space, and skip sc. In ch 5 loop, work: [sc, ch 3, sc, ch 5, sc, ch 3, sc]. Repeat from * 4 times, and from * to ** once more. Join with sl st in initial ch 1.
Rnd 4: sl st in ch 3 loop, and ch 1 (counts as sc). *ch 3. [sc, ch 5, sc] in next ch 5 loop. ch 3, and sc in next ch 3 loop. ch 4. Skip sc, and skip ch 2 space. tr in 4 tr. ch 4.** Skip ch 2 space, and skip sc. sc in ch 3 loop. Repeat from * 4 times, and from * to ** once more. Join with sl st in initial ch 1.
Rnd 5: sl st in ch 3 loop, and ch 3 (counts as dc). *In next ch 5 loop, work: [sc, ch 3, sc, ch 4, sc, ch 3, sc]. dc in next ch 3 loop. ch 3. Skip sc, skip ch 4 space, and skip 1 tr. sc in 1 tr, ch 2, and sc in next tr. ch 3. Skip tr, skip ch 4 space, and skip sc.** dc in ch 3 loop. Repeat from * 4 times, and from * to ** once more. Join with sl st in top of initial ch 3. Fasten off; weave in ends.

○ = ch   • = sl st   + = sc   ⊢—— = dc   ⊢—✕— = tr

39 Flowering Hexagon

Finished diameter: 3 in (76 mm)

Thread required: 12 yds (11.0 m)

Foundation ring: ch 6, and join with sl st in first ch.

Rnd 1: ch 1 (counts as sc). 11 sc in ring. Join with sl st in initial ch 1.

Rnd 2: ch 4 (counts as tr). *ch 3. 4-tr cluster in 1 sc. ch 3.** tr in 1 sc. Repeat from * 4 times, and from * to ** once more. Join with sl st in top of initial ch 4.

Rnd 3: ch 1 (counts as sc). ch 4, and sc in same ch as last sl st. *ch 3, and dc in top of next tr cluster. ch 5, and sl st in top of last dc made, to form loop. ch 3.** [sc, ch 4, sc] in next tr. Repeat from * 4 times, and from * to ** once more. Join with sl st in initial ch 1.

Rnd 4: sl st in ch 4 loop, and ch 4 (counts as tr). [tr, ch 2, 2-tr cluster] in same loop. *ch 2, and 2-tr cluster in next ch 5 loop (at point). [ch 2, 2-tr cluster] 3 times in same loop.** [ch 2, 2-tr cluster] twice in next ch 4 loop (halfway between points). Repeat from * 4 times, and from * to ** once more. ch 2. Skip initial ch 4, and join with sl st in top of initial tr.

Rnd 5: sl st in next ch 2 space, and ch 1 (counts as sc). [ch 3, sc] in each of the next 2 ch 2 spaces, skipping the tr clusters between them. *ch 3. [sc, ch 3, sc] in next ch 2 space.** [ch 3, sc] in each of the next 5 ch 2 spaces. Repeat from * 4 times, and from * to ** once more. [ch 3, sc] in each of the next 2 ch 2 spaces. ch 3, and join with sl st in initial ch 1. Fasten off; weave in ends.

○ = ch   • = sl st   + = sc   ⊢— = dc   ⊢⧸— = tr

40 Swirled Hexagon

Finished diameter: 3 in (76 mm)

Thread required: 13 yds (11.9 m)

Foundation ring: ch 4, and join with sl st in first ch.

Rnd 1: ch 1 (counts as sc). [ch 8, sc] 5 times in ring. ch 8, and join with sl st in initial ch 1.

Rnd 2: sl st in 2 ch, and in ch 8 loop. ch 1 (counts as sc), and 3 sc in same loop. *ch 3. 4 sc in next ch 8 loop. Repeat from * 4 times. ch 3, and join with sl st in initial ch 1.

Rnd 3: ch 1 (counts as sc). sc in 3 sc. *3 sc in ch 3 space.** sc in 4 sc. Repeat from * 4 times, and from * to ** once more. Join with sl st in initial ch 1.

Rnd 4: sl st in 1 sc, and ch 1 (counts as sc). *ch 3. sc in next sc. ch 6.** Skip 5 sc, and sc in 1 sc. Repeat from * 4 times, and from * to ** once more. Join with sl st in initial ch 1.

Rnd 5: sl st in ch 3 loop. ch 1 (counts as sc). *[ch 8, sc] 3 times in same ch 3 loop. 5 sc in next ch 6 space.** sc in next ch 3 loop. Repeat from * 4 times, and from * to ** once more. Join with sl st in initial ch 1.

Rnd 6: sl st in 2 ch, and in ch 8 loop. ch 1 (counts as sc), and 3 sc in same loop. *[ch 3; 4 sc in next ch 8 loop] twice.** 4 sc in next ch 8 loop. Repeat from * 4 times, and from * to ** once more. Join with sl st in initial ch 1.

Rnd 7: sl st in 1 sc, and ch 1 (counts as sc). sc in 2 sc. *2 sc in ch 3 space. sc in 1 sc. ch 4. Skip 2 sc, and sc in 1 sc. 2 sc in ch 3 space. sc in 3 sc. ch 2.** Skip 2 sc, and sc in 3 sc. Repeat from * 4 times, and from * to ** once more. Join with sl st in initial ch 1. Fasten off; weave in ends.

○ = ch • = sl st + = sc

41 Sunflower Hexagon

Finished diameter: 3 in (76 mm)
Thread required: 12 yds (11.0 m)

Foundation ring: ch 6, and join with sl st in first ch.
Rnd 1: ch 3 (counts as dc). 11 dc in ring. Join with sl st in top of initial ch 3.
Rnd 2: ch 1 (counts as sc). [ch 3, sc] in each of the remaining 11 dc. ch 3, and join with sl st in initial ch 1.
Rnd 3: sl st in ch 3 space, and ch 4 (counts as tr). 2-tr cluster in same ch 3 space. [ch 5, 3-tr cluster] in each of the 11 remaining ch 3 spaces. ch 5, and join with sl st in top of initial cluster.
Rnd 4: sl st in ch 5 space, and ch 1 (counts as sc). In same space, work: [sc, hdc, ch 2, hdc, 2 sc, ch 1]. In each of the 11 remaining ch 5 spaces, work: [2 sc, hdc, ch 2, hdc, 2 sc, ch 1]. Join with sl st in initial ch 1.
Rnd 5: sl st in sc, in hdc, and in ch 2 point. ch 1 (counts as sc). ch 3, and dc in next ch 1 space (halfway between points). *ch 3. [dc, ch 3, dc] in next ch 2 point. ch 3, and dc in next ch 1 space.** ch 3, and sc in next ch 2 point. ch 3, and dc in next ch 1 space. Repeat from * 4 times, and from * to ** once more. ch 3, and join with sl st in initial ch 1.
Rnd 6: sl st in 1 ch, and in ch 3 space. ch 1 (counts as sc). [ch 3, sc] in 1 ch 3 space. *ch 3. [sc, ch 2, sc] in next ch 3 space (at point).** [ch 3, sc] in each of 4 ch 3 spaces. Repeat from * 4 times, and from * to ** once more. [ch 3, sc] in each of 2 ch 3 spaces. ch 3, and join with sl st in initial ch 1. Fasten off; weave in ends.

○ = ch • = sl st + = sc ├── = hdc ├─╫─ = dc ├─╫─ = tr

42 Branch

Finished height: 3¼ in (83 mm)

Thread required: 5 yds (4.6 m)

ch 10. *ch 8, and sl st in 8th ch from hook to form loop. Bypass the stem, passing the thread under it, and work in the ch 8 loop: [3 sc, hdc, ch 1, dc, ch 1, dc, ch 4 and sl st in 3rd ch from hook to form picot, ch 1, dc, ch 1, dc, ch 1, hdc, 3 sc]. sl st in the ch at the base of the leaf, and in the next 3 ch.** ch 11, and repeat from * to **. ch 8, and repeat from * to **. Continuing down the branch, sl st in 1 ch. ch 3, and repeat from * to **. sc in next 8 ch of branch (working only in empty ch, and skipping the bases of the opposite leaf stems). ch 3, and repeat from * to **. sc in next 7 ch, hdc in 1 ch, dc in 2 ch, and tr in 1 ch (again working only in empty stitches). Fasten off; weave in ends.

○ = ch ·= sl st + = sc ├── = hdc ├─/ = dc ├─//─ = tr

43 Holly

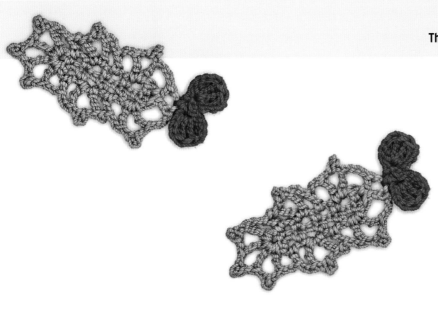

Finished length: 2³⁄₄ in (70 mm)
Thread required: color A, 3 yds (2.7 m); color B, 1 yd (0.9 m)

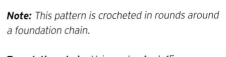

Note: *This pattern is crocheted in rounds around a foundation chain.*

Foundation chain: Using color A, ch 15.
Rnd 1: sc in 4th ch from hook. Continuing down chain, *ch 2, skip 2 ch, and sc in 1 ch.** Repeat from * to ** twice. ch 2. Skip 1 ch. [sc, ch 3, sc] in 1 ch (at end). Working around other side of chain, ch 2, skip 1 ch, and sc in 1 ch. Repeat from * to ** 3 times. Join with sl st in ch 3 point.
Rnd 2: ch 3 (counts as dc), ch 3, and dc in same ch 3 point. ch 3. *In next ch 2 space, work: [tr, ch 4 and sl st in 3rd ch from hook for picot, ch 1, tr]. ch 2, and dc in next ch 2 space. ch 2.** Repeat from * to ** once. tr in ch 3 point. [ch 4 and sl st in 3rd ch from hook, ch 1, tr] 3 times in same ch 3 point. ch 2, and dc in next ch 2 space. ch 2. Repeat from * to **. In next ch 2 space, work: [tr, ch 4 and sl st in 3rd ch from hook for picot, ch 1, tr]. ch 3, and join with sl st in top of initial ch 3. Fasten off color A.
Berries: Attach color B in ch 3 space at the bottom of the leaf. ch 1. *ch 5. In 1st ch of ch 5, work: [2 2-tr clusters, ch 4, sl st]. sl st in initial ch 1. Repeat from * once. Fasten off; weave in ends.

Color A

Color B

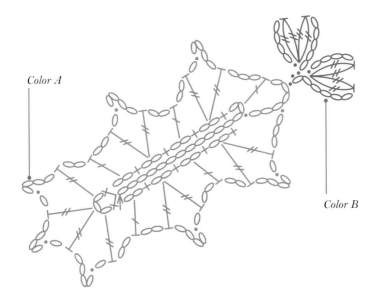

○ = ch • = sl st + = sc ⊢—— = dc ⊢—— = tr ⇒ = Beginning of leaf

44 Scallop Shell

Finished height: 1½ in (38 mm)

Thread required: 5 yds (4.6 m)

Foundation ring: ch 5, and join with sl st in first ch.

Rnd 1: ch 1 (counts as sc). 7 sc in ring. Join with sl st in initial ch 1.

Rnd 2: ch 2. sc in 1 sc. ch 2. 2 tr in each of 5 sc. ch 2. sc in 1 sc. ch 2. Join with sl st in sl st.

Rnd 3: ch 1. sc in ch 2 space, and in sc. 2 sc in ch 2 space. ch 2. dc in 1 tr. 2 tr in 1 tr. *ch 7. 2 tr in 1 tr. Repeat from * 6 times. dc in 1 tr. ch 2. 2 sc in ch 2 space. sc in sc, and in ch 2 space. ch 1. sc in sl st.

Rnd 4: ch 2. Skip ch 1 space, and skip 1 sc. sc in 1 sc. ch 3, and sl st in 2 sc, in ch 2 space, in dc, and in tr. ch 3, and tr in next tr. *3 sc in ch 7 space.** 2-tr decrease in 2 tr. Repeat from * 5 times, and from * to ** once more. tr in 1 tr. ch 3. sl st in tr, in dc, in ch 2 space, and in 2 sc. ch 3. sc in 1 sc. ch 2. Skip sc, and skip ch 1 space. Join with sl st in sc. Fasten off; weave in ends.

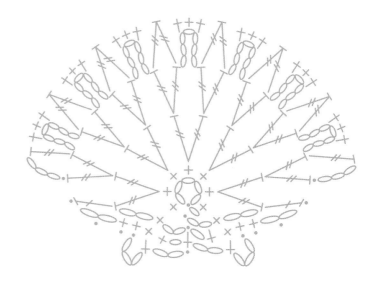

○ = ch • = sl st + = sc ┣──┫ = dc ┣─╫─┫ = tr

45 Sand Dollar

Finished height: 2 in (51 mm)

Thread required: 6 yds (5.5 m)

Foundation ring: ch 4, and join with sl st in first ch.

Rnd 1: ch 1 (counts as sc). [ch 9, sc] in ring. [ch 14, sc] in ring. [ch 18, sc] in ring. [ch 14, sc] in ring. [ch 9, sc] in ring. sc in ring. Join with sl st in initial ch 1.

Rnd 2: ch 3 (counts as dc). dc in same ch as last sl st. 4 sc in ch 9 loop. dc in sc, and ch 2. 4 sc in ch 14 loop. ch 2. tr in sc, and ch 3. 4 sc in ch 18 loop. ch 3. tr in sc, and ch 2. 4 sc in ch 14 loop. ch 2. dc in sc. 4 sc in ch 9 loop. 2 dc in 1 sc, and dc in 1 sc. Join with sl st in top of initial ch 3.

Rnd 3: ch 3 (counts as dc). dc in dc. sc in 4 sc. 3 dc in dc. Skip ch 2 space. sc in 3 sc. [sc, hdc, dc] in 1 sc. Skip ch 2 space, and 4 tr in tr. Skip ch 3 space. sc in 1 sc, 2 sc in each of 2 sc, and sc in 1 sc. Skip ch 3 space, and 4 tr in tr. Skip ch 2 space. [dc, hdc, sc] in 1 sc. sc in 3 sc. Skip ch 2 space. 3 dc in dc. sc in 4 sc. dc in 2 dc, and 2 dc in 1 dc. Join with sl st in top of initial ch 3.

Rnd 4: ch 1 (counts as sc). sc in each of 45 stitches. Join with sl st in initial ch 1. Fasten off; weave in ends.

○ = ch • = sl st + = sc ┠─ = hdc ┠╱ = dc ┠╱╱ = tr

46 Sun

Finished diameter: 3¼ in (83 mm)

Thread required: 10 yds (9.1 m)

Foundation ring: ch 8, and join with sl st in first ch.
Rnd 1: ch 1 (counts as sc). 15 sc in ring. Join with sl st in initial ch 1.
Rnd 2: ch 1 (counts as sc). [ch 3, sc] in each of 15 sc. ch 3, and join with sl st in intial ch 1.
Rnd 3: sl st 1 ch, and in ch 3 space. ch 3 (counts as dc). [ch 2, dc] in each of 15 ch 3 spaces. ch 2, and join with sl st in top of initial ch 3.
Rnd 4: sl st in ch 2 space, and ch 2 (counts as hdc). 2 hdc in same ch 2 space. 3 hdc in each of the 15 remaining ch 2 spaces. Join with sl st in top of initial ch 2.
Rnd 5: ch 1 (counts as sc). *ch 3. Skip 1 hdc, and sc in 2 hdc. Repeat from * 14 times. ch 3, skip 1 hdc, and sc in 1 hdc. Join with sl st in initial ch 1.
Rnd 6: *ch 3. dc in ch 3 space. ch 4, and sl st in top of last dc made for picot. ch 3, and sl st in next sc. ch 5. Skip sc, and dtr in ch 3 space. ch 5, and sl st in top of last dtr made for picot. ch 5.** Skip 1 sc, and sl st in 1 sc. Repeat from * 6 times, and from * to ** once more. Skip 1 sc, and join with sl st in sl st. Fasten off; weave in ends.

○ = ch •= sl st + = sc ⊢——⊣ = hdc ⊢⁄—— = dc ⊢—ⱨⱨⱨ—— = dtr

47 Moon

Finished height: 3 in (76 mm)

Thread required: 5 yds (4.6 m)

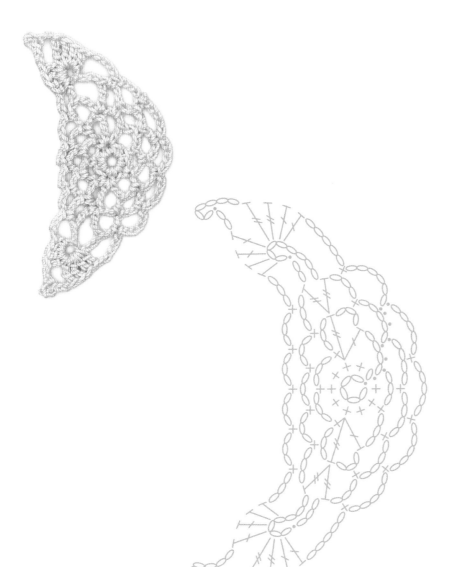

Foundation ring: ch 5, and join with sl st in first ch.

Rnd 1: ch 1 (counts as sc). 9 sc in ring. Join with sl st in initial ch 1.

Rnd 2: ch 1 (counts as sc). ch 3. Skip 1 sc. In next sc, work: [dc, ch 3, tr, ch 3, sc]. ch 3, skip 1 sc, and sc in 1 sc. ch 3. Skip 1 sc. In next sc, work: [sc, ch 3, tr, ch 3, dc]. ch 3, skip 1 sc, and sc in 1 sc. ch 3, and join with sl st in initial ch 1.

Rnd 3: sl st in 1 ch, and in ch 3 space. ch 1 (counts as sc). ch 4, and sc in next ch 3 space. ch 3. In tr, work: [tr, ch 8 and sl st in 5th ch from hook, ch 2, tr]. [ch 3, sc] in each of next 4 ch 3 spaces. ch 3. In tr, work: [tr, ch 7 and sl st in 5th ch from hook, ch 3, tr]. ch 3, and sc in ch 3 space. [ch 4, sc] in each of 2 ch 3 spaces. ch 4, and join with sl st in initial ch 1.

Rnd 4: sl st in 2 ch, and in ch 4 space. ch 1 (counts as sc). [ch 5, sc] in next ch 3 space. ch 5, and skip next ch 3 space. In ch 5 loop, work: [2 dc, 2 tr, ch 6 and sl st in 4th ch from hook for picot, ch 2, 2 dc, 2 hdc]. ch 3. Skip ch 2 space, and sc in ch 3 space. [ch 3, sc] in each of 4 ch 3 spaces. ch 3, and skip ch 2 space. In ch 5 loop, work: [2 hdc, 2 dc, ch 6 and sl st in 4th ch from hook, ch 2, 2 tr, 2 dc]. ch 5, skip 1 ch 3 space, and sc in next ch 3 space. [ch 5, sc] in each of 3 ch 4 spaces. ch 5, and join with sl st in initial ch 1. Fasten off; weave in ends.

48 Star-crossed Star

Finished diameter: 2 in (51 mm)

Thread required: 8 yds (7.3 m)

Foundation ring: ch 5, and join with sl st in first ch.

Rnd 1: ch 1 (counts as sc). 9 sc in ring. Join with sl st in initial ch 1.

Rnd 2: ch 1 (counts as sc). sc in 1 sc. *ch 3. sc in 2 sc. Repeat from * 3 times. ch 3, and join with sl st in initial ch 1.

Rnd 3: sl st in sc, and in ch 3 point. ch 3 (counts as dc). 4-dc cluster in same ch 3 point. *ch 6. 5-dc cluster in next ch 3 point. Repeat from * 3 times. ch 6, and join with sl st in top of initial dc cluster.

Rnd 4: sl st in next ch 6 space, and ch 1 (counts as sc). In same ch 6 space, work: [hdc, dc, tr, dtr, ch 2, dtr, tr, dc, hdc, sc]. In each of the 4 remaining ch 6 spaces, work: [sc, hdc, dc, tr, dtr, ch 2, dtr, tr, dc, hdc, sc]. Join with sl st in initial ch 1.

Rnd 5: *sc in next 4 stitches. [sc, ch 2, sc] in ch 2 point. sc in next 4 stitches.** sl st in 2 sc. Repeat from * 3 times, and from * to ** once. sl st in 1 sc, and join with sl st in sl st. Fasten off; weave in ends.

49 Leafy Square

Finished width: 2 in (51 mm)
Thread required: 10 yds (9.1 m)

Foundation ring: ch 6, and join with sl st in first ch.
Rnd 1: ch 3 (counts as dc). 15 dc in ring. Join with sl st in top of initial ch 3.
Rnd 2: *ch 7. sl st in 5th ch from hook to form loop. Bypass stem (pass thread under stem), and work the following stitches into the loop: [3 sc, hdc, ch 3, hdc, 3 sc]. sl st in same ch as last sl st (at the base of the loop), and in the 2nd ch of the last ch 7.** Repeat from * to **. sl st in next 2 empty ch (the 1st ch of the last ch 7, and the 1st ch of the previous ch 7).*** Back on main ring, sl st in 4 dc. Repeat from * twice, and from * to *** once more. sl st in 3 dc.
Rnd 3: ch 4 (counts as tr). *ch 8. Skip 1 leaf (pass chain behind it), and sc in ch 3 point of next leaf. ch 8.** Skip the rest of the leaf and stem, and tr in 3rd sl st on main ring. Repeat from * twice, and from * to ** once more. Join with sl st in top of initial ch 4.
Rnd 4: sl st in ch 8 space, and ch 3 (counts as dc). 7 dc in same space. *[2 dc, ch 3, 2 dc] in sc.** 8 dc in each of the next 2 ch 8 spaces. Repeat from * twice, and from * to ** once more. 8 dc in ch 8 space. Join with sl st in top of initial ch 3. Fasten off; weave in ends.

○ = ch   • = sl st   + = sc   ├── = hdc   ├╫── = dc   ├╫── = tr

50 Lace Heart

Finished height: 2³⁄₈ in (60 mm)
Thread required: 7 yds (6.4 m)

Foundation ring: ch 6, and join with sl st in first ch.
Rnd 1: ch 5. 6 tr in ring. ch 3. 6 tr in ring. ch 5. sl st in ring.
Rnd 2: 5 sc in ch 5 space. hdc in 1 tr. dc in 5 tr. [2 dc, tr, ch 2, tr, 2 dc] in ch 3 space. dc in 5 tr. hdc in 1 tr. 5 sc in ch 5 space. Join with sl st in sl st.
Rnd 3: ch 6. Skip 3 sc, and dc in 1 sc. [ch 3, skip 1 stitch, and dc in 1 stitch] 4 times. ch 3. In ch 2 point: [2 dc, ch 4 and sl st in 4th ch from hook to form loop, 2 dc]. ch 3. Skip 2 stitches, and dc in 1 stitch. [ch 3, skip 1 stitch, and dc in 1 stitch] 4 times. ch 6. Skip 3 sc. sl st over sl st, and into the sl st below.
Rnd 4: ch 6. sc in ch 6 space. [ch 4, dc] in each of the next 5 ch 3 spaces. ch 2. [2 sc, ch 2, 2 sc] in ch 4 loop. ch 2. dc in ch 3 space. [ch 4, dc] in each of the next 4 ch 3 spaces. ch 4, and sc in ch 6 space. ch 6. sl st over sl st, and into the sl st in Rnd 2.
Rnd 5: ch 6. sc in ch 6 space. [ch 5, sc] in each of the next 5 ch 4 spaces. ch 5. Skip dc, and skip ch 2 space. sc in 2 sc. ch 4, and sl st in 3rd ch from hook to form picot. ch 1. Skip ch 2 point. sc in 2 sc. Skip ch 2 space, and skip dc. [ch 5, sc] in 5 ch 4 spaces, and in ch 6 space. ch 6. sl st over sl st, and into the sl st in Rnd 2. Fasten off; weave in ends.

○ = ch • = sl st + = sc ⊢ = hdc ⊢— = dc ⊢╫— = tr ➤ = sl st over sl st, and into the sl st in Rnd 2

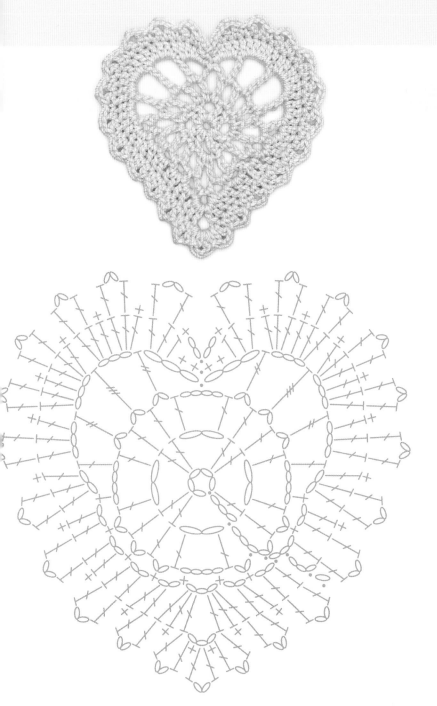

51 Ruffled Heart

Finished height: 2³⁄₄ in (70 mm)
Thread required: 10 yds (9.1 m)

Foundation ring: ch 5, and join with sl st in first ch.
Rnd 1: ch 3 (counts as dc). dc in ring. * ch 2. 2 dc in ring. Repeat from * twice. ch 2, and join with sl st in top of initial ch 3.
Rnd 2: ch 3 (counts as dc). [ch 2, dc] in next dc. *ch 2. [dc, ch 4, dc] in ch 2 point.** [ch 2, dc] in each of 2 dc. Repeat from * twice, and from * to ** once more. ch 2, and join with sl st in top of initial ch 3.
Rnd 3: sl st in ch 2 space, and ch 1 (counts as sc). [ch 2, sc] in next ch 2 space. [ch 2, sc, ch 2, dc] in ch 4 space. [ch 3, tr] in 1 ch 2 space. [ch 3, dtr] in 1 ch 2 space. [ch 3, tr] in 1 ch 2 space. [ch 3, sl st] in ch 4 space. [ch 3, tr] in 1 ch 2 space. [ch 3, dtr] in 1 ch 2 space. [ch 3, tr] in 1 ch 2 space. [ch 3, dc, ch 2, sc] in ch 4 space. [ch 2, sc] in each of 3 ch 2 spaces. ch 2. [sc, ch 3, sc] in ch 4 space. [ch 2, sc] in ch 2 space. ch 2, and join with sl st in initial ch 1.
Rnd 4: sl st in ch 2 space, and ch 3 (counts as dc). dc in same ch 2 space. 2 dc in 1 ch 2 space. 3 dc in next ch 2 space, and in 1 ch 3 space. 6 dc in each of 2 ch 3 spaces. [2 dc, hdc, 2 sc] in ch 3 space, and sl st in sl st. [2 sc, hdc, 2 dc] in 1 ch 3 space. 6 dc in each of 2 ch 3 spaces. 3 dc in ch 3 space, and in 1 ch 2 space. 2 dc in each of 4 ch 2 spaces. [3 dc, ch 3, 3 dc] in ch 3 point. 2 dc in each of 2 ch 2 spaces. Join with sl st in top of initial ch 3.
Rnd 5: ch 1 (counts as sc). *dc in 1 stitch, ch 2, and dc in next stitch. sc in 1 stitch.** Repeat from * to ** 7 times. ch 2. Skip 2 sc, and sl st in sl st. ch 2. Skip 2 sc, and sc in hdc. Repeat from * to ** 10 times. dc in 1 dc. ch 2. In ch 3 point, work: [dc, sc, dc, ch 2, dc, sc, dc]. ch 2. dc in 1 dc, and sc in 1 sc. Repeat from * to ** once, dc in 1 dc, ch 2, and dc in next dc. Join with sl st in initial ch 1. Fasten off; weave in ends.

○ = ch • = sl st ├── = hdc ├─── = dc ├─// = tr ├─/// = dtr

52 Floral Heart

Finished height: 4 in (102 mm)

Thread required: color A, 9 yds (8.2 m); color B, 16 yds (14.6 m)

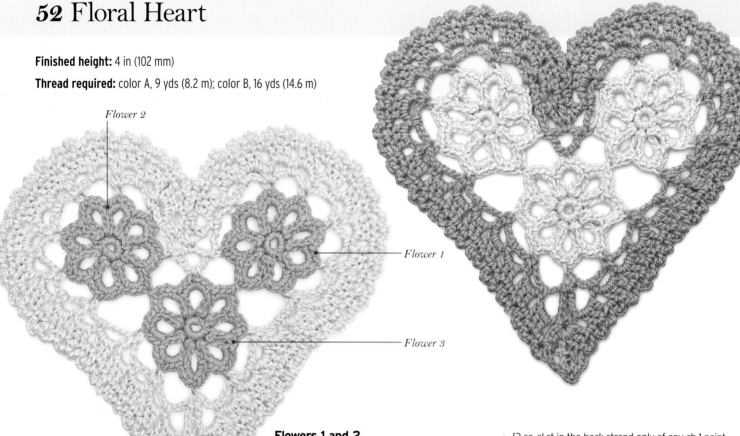

Flower 2

Flower 1

Flower 3

Flowers 1 and 2

Foundation ring: Using color A, ch 5, and join with sl st in first ch.

Rnd 1: ch 1 (counts as sc). 7 sc in ring. Join with sl st in initial ch 1.

Rnd 2: ch 8 and sl st in same ch as last sl st. [sl st, ch 8, sl st] in each of the 7 remaining sc. Join with sl st in sl st.

Rnd 3: sl st in 1 ch, and in ch 8 loop. ch 1 (counts as sc). [2 sc, ch 1, 3 sc] in same loop. [3 sc, ch 1, 3 sc] in each of the 7 remaining loops. Join with sl st in initial ch 1. Fasten off.

Flower 3

Repeat instructions for Flowers 1 and 2, with the following changes. In the 2nd petal of Rnd 3, work: [3 sc, sl st in the back strand only of any ch 1 point of Flower 1, 3 sc]. In the 4th petal of Rnd 3, work:

[3 sc, sl st in the back strand only of any ch 1 point of Flower 2, 3 sc].

Lace

Rnd 1: Work this round in the back strands only of the the flowers' outside rounds. Using color B, sc in the ch 1 point of the 7th petal of Flower 3. [ch 7, sc] in each of the next 2 ch 1 points of the same flower, and in the next 7 empty ch 1 points of Flower 1. [tr, ch 3, tr] in the next empty ch 1 point of Flower 3. sc in the next empty point of Flower 2. [ch 7, sc] in the next 6 points of Flower 2, and in the remaining 2 points of Flower 1. ch 7, and join with sl st in initial sc.

Rnd 2: ch 4 (counts as tr). ch 4, and sl st in 4th ch from hook to form loop. tr in same sc as initial sl st. *[ch 4, sc] in ch 7 space. [ch 4, sc] in sc.** Repeat from * to ** 7 times. [ch 4, sc] in ch 7 space. Skip sc, and skip tr. [ch 4, sc] in ch 3 space. Skip tr, and skip sc.

Color A

Color B

Repeat from * to ** 8 times. [ch 4, sc] in ch 7 space.
ch 4, and join with sl st in top of initial ch 4.
Rnd 3: sl st in ch 4 loop, and ch 3 (counts as dc). In
same loop work: [2 dc, ch 4 and sl st in 4th ch from
hook for loop, 3 dc]. *ch 1. 3 dc in next ch 4 space.**
Repeat from * to ** 16 times. ch 1. dc in ch 4 space,
in sc, and in ch 4 space. Repeat from * to ** 17
times. ch 1, and join with sl st in top of initial ch 3.
Rnd 4: sl st in dc, and ch 1 (counts as sc). ch 3.
Skip dc, and [sc, ch 3, sc] in ch 4 loop. *ch 3. Skip
1 dc, and sc in 1 dc. ch 3. Skip 1 dc and sc in ch 1
space.** Repeat from * to ** 17 times, skip 3 dc,
and sc in next ch 1 space. Repeat from * to **
17 times. ch 3, and join with sl st in initial ch 1.
Fasten off; weave in ends.

○ = ch   • = sl st   + = sc   ⊢—⊣ = dc   ⊢—⊣ = tr   ⊂ = work in back strand of stitch below   ➔ = beginning of flower or heart

53 Floating-flower Square

Finished width: 2 in (51 mm)

Thread required: color A, 7 yds (6.4 m); color B, 7 yds (6.4 m)

Foundation ring: Using color A, ch 8, and join with sl st in first ch.

Rnd 1: ch 1 (counts as sc). 15 sc in ring. Join with sl st in initial ch 1.

Rnd 2: *ch 5. 2 tr in 1 sc. ch 5.** sl st in 1 sc. Repeat from * 6 times, and from * to ** once more. Join with sl st in sl st.

Rnd 3: *[3 sc, hdc] in ch 5 space. [dc, tr] in front strand only of 1 tr. [tr, dc] in front strand only of next tr. [hdc, 3 sc] in ch 5 space. sl st in sl st. Repeat from * 7 times. Fasten off color A.

Rnd 4: *Using color B, and working behind Rnd 3, sc in the back strands only of the next 2 tr of Rnd 2 (in the middle of the petal's back). ch 4. Repeat from * 7 times. Join with sl st in initial sc.

Rnd 5: ch 3 (counts as dc). dc in sc. *[2 dc, ch 3, 2 dc] in ch 4 space. dc in 2 sc. 4 dc in ch 4 space.** dc in 2 sc. Repeat from * twice, and from * to ** once more. Join with sl st in top of initial ch 3.

Rnd 6: ch 1 (counts as sc). sc in 3 dc. *[2 hdc, ch 2, 2 hdc] in ch 3 space. sc in 4 dc. ch 5. Skip 4 dc.** sc in 4 dc. Repeat from * twice, and from * to ** once more. Join with sl st in initial ch 1.

Rnd 7: sl st in 3 sc. *ch 3. Skip 2 hdc, and [sl st, ch 3, sl st] in ch 2 point. ch 3. Skip 2 hdc, and sl st in 1 sc. ch 4, and sl st in beginning of next ch 5 space. ch 4, and sl st at end of same space.** ch 4, skip 3 sc, and sl st in 1 sc. Repeat from * twice, and from * to ** once more. ch 4, skip 3 sl st, and join with sl st in sl st. Fasten off; weave in ends.

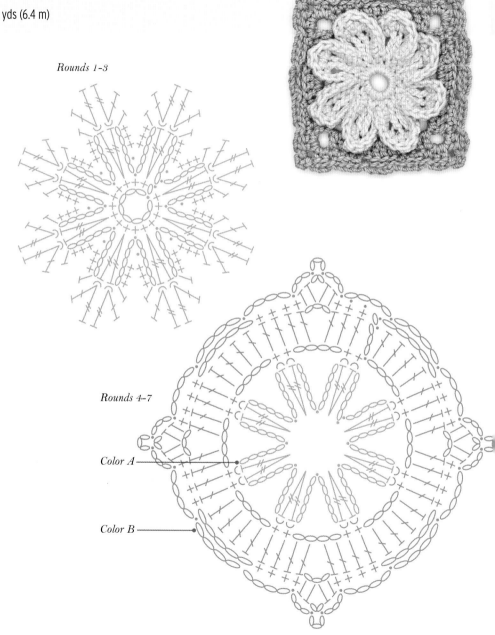

Rounds 1–3

Rounds 4–7

Color A ———

Color B ———

○ = ch   • = sl st   + = sc   ⊢— = dc   ⊢— = hdc   ⊢— = dc   ⊢— = tr   ⊃ = work stitch in front strand of stitch below   ⊂ = work stitch in back strand of stitch below

54 Filigree Medallion

Finished diameter: 3½ in (89 mm)
Thread required: 15 yds (13.7 m)

Foundation ring: ch 5, and join with sl st in first ch.
Rnd 1: ch 3 (counts as dc). dc in ring. *ch 3. 2 dc in ring. Repeat from * twice. ch 3, and join with sl st in top of initial ch 3.
Rnd 2: ch 1 (counts as sc). *ch 6 and sl st in 6th ch from hook for loop. sc in next dc. ch 2, and sc in ch 3 space. ch 2.** sc in next dc. Repeat from * twice, and from * to ** once more. Join with sl st in initial ch 1.
Rnd 3: sl st in ch 6 loop, and ch 3 (counts as dc). dc in same loop. *[ch 3, 2-dc cluster] 3 times in same loop. Skip sc, and skip ch 2 space. 5 tr in next sc. Skip ch 2 space, and skip sc.** 2-dc cluster in ch 6 loop. Repeat from * twice, and from * to ** once more. Skipping initial ch 3, join with sl st in initial dc.
Rnd 4: sl st in 1 ch, and in ch 3 space. ch 1 (counts as sc). *[ch 3, sc] in each of the next 2 ch 3 spaces. ch 5. Skip next dc cluster. 5-tr decrease in next 5 tr. ch 5.** Skip dc cluster, and sc in ch 3 space. Repeat from * twice, and from * to ** once more. Join with sl st in initial ch 1.
Rnd 5: sl st in ch 3 space, and ch 1 (counts as sc). [sc, ch 4, sc] in same ch 3 space. *[dc, tr, ch 2, tr, dc] in sc. [sc, ch 4, 2 sc] in next ch 3 space. [4 sc, ch 4, sc] in ch 5 space. [dc, tr, ch 2, tr, dc] in top of 5-tr decrease. [sc, ch 4, 4 sc] in ch 5 space.** [2 sc, ch 4, sc] in next ch 3 space. Repeat from * twice, and from * to ** once more. Join with sl st in initial ch 1.
Rnd 6: sl st in sc, in 1 ch, and in ch 4 loop. ch 1 (counts as sc). ch 4, and sc in same ch 4 loop. *ch 3. [sc, ch 5, sc] in next ch 2 point. ch 3. [sc, ch 4, sc] in next ch 4 loop. ch 3.** [sc, ch 4, sc] in the following ch 4 loop. Repeat from * 6 times, and from * to ** once more. Join with sl st in initial ch 1. Fasten off; weave in ends.

○ = ch • = sl st + = sc ⊢⟋⊣ = dc ⊢⟋⟋⊣ = tr

55 Vortex Doily

Finished diameter: 6¼ in (159 mm)

Thread required: 52 yds (47.5 m)

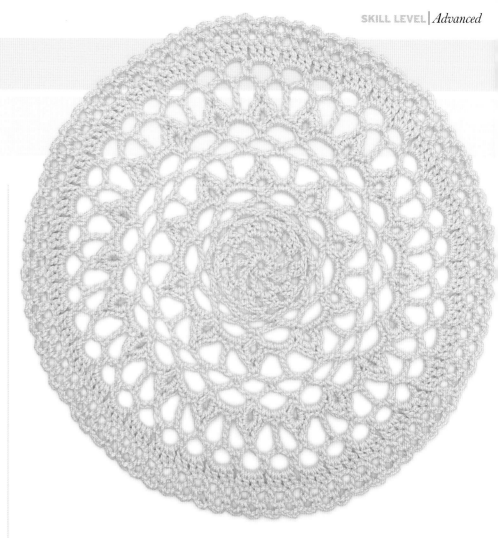

Foundation ring: ch 6, and join with sl st in first ch.

Rnd 1: ch 4 (counts as tr). [ch 2, tr] 9 times in ring. ch 2, and join with sl st in top of initial ch 4.

Rnd 2: sl st in ch 2 space, and ch 3 (counts as dc). dc in same space. *ch 2. 2 dc in next ch 2 space. Repeat from * 8 times. ch 2, and join with sl st in top of initial ch 3.

Rnd 3: sl st in dc, and in ch 2 space. ch 1 (counts as sc). [ch 4, sc] in each of the next 9 ch 2 spaces. ch 4, and join with sl st in initial ch 1.

Rnd 4: sl st in 1 ch, and in ch 4 space. ch 1 (counts as sc). [ch 5, sc] in each of the 9 remaining ch 4 spaces. ch 5. Join with sl st in initial ch 1.

Rnd 5: sl st in 2 ch, and in ch 5 space. ch 1 (counts as sc). ch 6, and sl st in last ch 1 made, to form loop. *ch 6. sc in next ch 5 space. ch 6, and sl st in top of last sc made, for loop. Repeat from * 8 times. ch 6, and join with sl st in initial ch 1.

Rnd 6: sl st in ch 6 loop, and ch 1 (counts as sc). [2 sc, ch 3, 3 sc] in same ch 6 loop. *4 sc in next ch 6 space.** [3 sc, ch 3, 3 sc] in next ch 6 loop. Repeat from * 8 times, and from * to ** once more. Join with sl st in initial ch 1.

Rnd 7: sl st in 2 sc, and in ch 3 point. ch 1 (counts as sc). *ch 4. Skip 5 sc, and tr in 1 sc. ch 4.** sc in next ch 3 point. Repeat from * 8 times, and from * to ** once more. Join with sl st in initial ch 1.

Rnd 8: sl st in 1 ch, and in ch 4 space. ch 1 (counts as sc). [ch 5, sc] in each of the 19 remaining ch 4 spaces. ch 5. Join with sl st in initial ch 1.

Rnd 9: sl st in 2 ch, and in ch 5 space. ch 1 (counts as sc). ch 6, and sl st in last ch 1 made, to form loop. *ch 6. sc in next ch 5 space. ch 6, and sl st in top of last sc made, for loop. Repeat from * 18 times. ch 6, and join with sl st in initial ch 1.

Rnd 10: sl st in ch 6 loop, and ch 1 (counts as sc). [2 sc, ch 3, 3 sc] in same ch 6 loop. *4 sc in next ch 6 space.** [3 sc, ch 3, 3 sc] in next ch 6 loop.

Repeat from * 18 times, and from * to ** once more. Join with sl st in initial ch 1.

Rnd 11: sl st in 2 sc, and in ch 3 point. ch 1 (counts as sc). *ch 4. Skip 5 sc, and tr in 1 sc. ch 4.** sc in next ch 3 point. Repeat from * 18 times, and from * to ** once more. Join with sl st in initial ch 1.

Rnd 12: sl st in 1 ch, and in ch 4 space. ch 1 (counts as sc). [ch 5, sc] in each of the 39 remaining ch 4 spaces. ch 5. Join with sl st in initial ch 1.

Rnd 13: sl st in next ch 5 space, and ch 3 (counts as dc). [dc, ch 1, 2 dc] in the same space. [ch 1, 2 dc, ch 1, 2 dc] in each of the 39 remaining ch 5 spaces. ch 1, and join with sl st in 3rd ch of initial ch 3.

Rnd 14: ch 1 (counts as sc). *ch 3. Skip dc, skip ch, and sc in 1 dc. Repeat from * 78 times. ch 3, and join with sl st in initial ch 1.

Rnd 15: sl st in next ch, and in ch 3 space. ch 1 (counts as sc). [ch 3, sc] in each of the 79 remaining spaces. ch 3, and join with sl st in initial ch 1. Fasten off; weave in ends.

○ = ch   ·= sl st   + = sc   ⊢×— = dc   ⊢×× = tr

56 Scallop-edged Doily

Finished diameter: 6 in (152 mm)

Thread required: 47 yds (43.0 m)

Foundation ring: ch 7, and join with sl st in first ch.

Rnd 1: ch 3 (counts as dc). 15 dc in ring. Join with sl st in top of initial ch 3.

Rnd 2: ch 1 (counts as sc). *ch 4. Skip 1 dc, and sc in 1 dc. Repeat from * 6 times. ch 4, and join with sl st in initial ch 1.

Rnd 3: sl st in next ch 4 space, and ch 4 (counts as tr). 3-tr cluster in same ch 4 space. *ch 7. 4-tr cluster in next ch 4 space. Repeat from * 6 times. ch 7, and join with sl st in top of initial cluster.

Rnd 4: ch 3 (counts as dc). ch 3, and dc in same cluster as last sl st. *ch 3. In the middle of the next ch 7 space, work: [sc, ch 4 and sl st in 4th ch from hook to form loop, sc]. ch 3.** [dc, ch 3, dc] in top of next tr cluster. Repeat from * 6 times, and from * to ** once more. Join with sl st in top of initial ch 3.

Rnd 5: sl st in ch 3 point, and ch 4 (counts as tr). 5 tr in same ch 3 point. *ch 2. sc in next ch 4 loop (between tr groups). ch 2.** Skip 1 ch 3 space, and 6 tr in next ch 3 point. Repeat from * 6 times, and from * to ** once more. Join with sl st in top of initial ch 4.

Rnd 6: ch 1 (counts as sc). *[ch 2, sc] in each of 5 tr. ch 4. Skip ch 2 space, skip sc, and skip next ch 2 space.** sc in next tr. Repeat from * 6 times, and from * to ** once more. Join with sl st in initial ch 1.

Rnd 7: sl st in ch 2 space, and ch 1 (counts as sc). *[ch 2, sc] in each of the next 4 ch 2 spaces.** [ch 2, sc] in ch 4 space, and in ch 2 space. Repeat from * 6 times, and from * to ** once more. [ch 2, sc] in ch 4 space. ch 2, and join with sl st in initial ch 1.

Rnd 8: sl st in ch 2 space, and ch 1 (counts as sc). *[ch 2, sc] in each of the next 3 ch 2 spaces. ch 4. Skip sc, and skip ch 2 space. sc in sc. ch 4. Skip ch 2 space, and skip sc.** sc in next ch 2 space. Repeat from * 6 times, and from * to ** once more. Join with sl st in initial ch 1.

Rnd 9: sl st in ch 2 space, and ch 1 (counts as sc). *[ch 2, sc] in each of the next 2 ch 2 spaces. ch 6. Skip sc, and skip ch 4 space. sc in sc. ch 6. Skip ch 4 space, and skip sc.** sc in next ch 2 space. Repeat from * 6 times, and from * to ** once more. Join with sl st in initial ch 1.

Rnd 10: sl st in ch 2 space, and ch 1 (counts as sc). *[ch 2, sc] in next ch 2 space. ch 8. Skip sc, and skip ch 6 space. sc in sc. ch 8. Skip ch 6 space, and skip sc.** sc in next ch 2 space. Repeat from * 6 times, and from * to ** once more. Join with sl st in initial ch 1.

Rnd 11: sl st in ch 2 space, and ch 1 (counts as sc). *ch 6, and sl st in 6th ch from hook for loop. sc in same ch 2 space. ch 4. [sc, ch 3, sc] in middle of ch 8 space. ch 4. dc in next sc. ch 5, and sl st in top of last dc made for loop. ch 4. [sc, ch 3, sc] in middle of ch 8 space. ch 4.** sc in next ch 2 space. Repeat from * 6 times, and from * to ** once more. Join with sl st in initial ch 1.

Rnd 12: sl st in ch 6 loop, and ch 3 (counts as dc). [dc, ch 2, 2 dc] in same loop. *ch 3, skip ch 4 space, and sc in next ch 3 loop. ch 3, skip ch 4 space, and [2 dc, ch 2, 2 dc] in next ch 5 loop. ch 3, skip ch 4 space, and sc in next ch 3 loop. ch 3.** Skip ch 4 space, and [2 dc, ch 2, 2 dc] in next ch 6 loop. Repeat from * 6 times, and from * to ** once more. Join with sl st in top of initial ch 3.

Rnd 13: ch 3 (counts as dc). dc in dc. *4 dc in ch 2 point. dc in 2 dc. [ch 2, sc] in each of the next 2 ch 3 spaces. ch 2.** dc in 2 dc. Repeat from * 14 times, and from * to ** once more. Join with sl st in top of initial ch 3.

Rnd 14: ch 1 (counts as sc). *hdc in 1 dc, and dc in 2 dc. ch 2. dc in 2 dc, hdc in 1 dc, and sc in 1 dc. ch 2. Skip 1 ch 2 space, and sc in next ch 2 space. ch 2.** Skip next ch 2 space. sc in dc. Repeat from * 14 times, and from * to ** once more. Join with sl st in initial ch 1. Fasten off; weave in ends.

○ = ch • = sl st + = sc ⊢— = hdc ⊢—⁄ = dc ⊢—⁄⁄ = tr

57 Garden Hexagon

Finished diameter: 2 in (51 mm)

Thread required: color A, 1 yd (0.9 m); color B, 4 yds (3.7 m); color C, 14 yds (12.8 m)

Foundation ring: Using color A, ch 6 and join with sl st in first ch.
Rnd 1: ch 1 (counts as sc). 11 sc in ring. Using color B, join with sl st in initial ch 1. Continue with B.
Rnd 2: *ch 7. Starting in 3rd ch from hook and continuing down chain, dc in 1 ch, tr in 2 ch, dc in 1 ch, and sc in 1 ch.** Back on ring, sl st in front strand only of 1 sc. Repeat from * 10 times, and from * to ** once more. Join with sl st in sl st. Fasten off color B.
Rnd 3: Work this round behind Rnd 2, into the back strands of Rnd 1. Using color C, work 2 sc in each of 12 stitches. Join with sl st in initial sc.
Rnd 4: ch 1 (counts as sc). *ch 2. Skip 1 sc, and sc in 1 sc. Repeat from * 10 times. ch 2, and join with sl st in initial ch 1.
Rnd 5: sl st in ch 2 space, and ch 1 (counts as sc). ch 2. sl st in the back strand only of the tr closest to the center of the nearest flower petal (you will be working into a tr in Rnd 2). ch 2. *Returning to Rnd 4, sc in next ch 2 space. ch 2, and sl st in the back strand only of the centermost tr of the next flower petal. ch 2. Repeat from * 10 times. Join with sl st in initial ch 1.
Rnd 6: ch 1 (counts as sc). *ch 4. Skip ch 2 space, skip sl st, and skip ch 2 space.** sc in sc. Repeat from * 10 times, and from * to ** once more. Join with sl st in initial ch 1.
Rnd 7: ch 1 (counts as sc). *ch 2. dc in next ch 4 space. ch 4, and sl st in top of last dc made, to form loop. ch 2, and sc in next sc. ch 2. sc in next ch 4 space. ch 2.** sc in sc. Repeat from * 4 times, and from * to ** once more. Join with sl st in initial ch 1.
Rnd 8: sl st in 2 ch, in dc, and in ch 4 loop. ch 2 (counts as hdc). [3 hdc, ch 2, 4 hdc] in same ch 4 loop. *ch 3. Skip sl st, skip ch 2 space, skip sc, and skip ch 2 space. [sc, ch 6, sc] in 1 sc (halfway between points). ch 3.** [4 hdc, ch 2, 4 hdc] in next ch 4 loop (at point). Repeat from * 4 times, and from * to ** once more. Join with sl st in top of initial ch 2.
Rnd 9: *[ch 2, sl st] in each of 3 hdc. ch 2. [sl st, ch 3, sl st] in ch 2 point. [ch 2, sl st] in each of 4 hdc. ch 2. Skip ch 3 space, and sl st in sc. [4 sc, ch 2, 4 sc] in ch 6 loop. sl st in sc. ch 2.** Skip ch 3 space, and sl st in sc. Repeat from * 4 times, and from * to ** once more. Join with sl st in sl st. Fasten off; weave in ends.

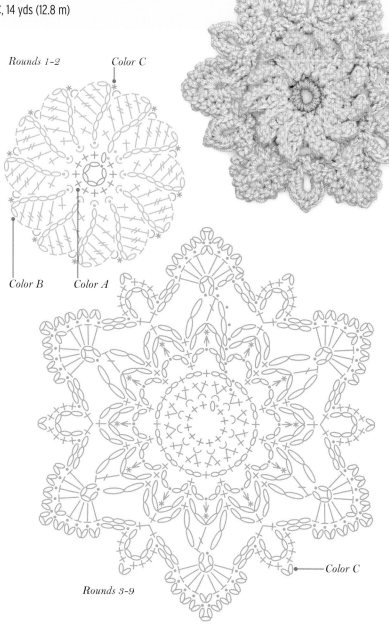

Rounds 1-2   *Color C*

Color B   *Color A*

Color C

Rounds 3-9

○ = ch   ꞏ = sl st   + = sc   ┝─┥ = dc   ┝═┥ = tr   ⊃ = work in front strand of stitch below   ⊂ = work in back strand of stitch below   ✳◄·— = sl st in Rnd 2, in st marked with *

58 Offset-snowflake Hexagon

Finished diameter: 3 in (76 mm)

Thread required: color A, 6 yds (5.5 m); color B, 6 yds (5.5 m)

Foundation ring: Using color A, ch 6 and join with sl st in first ch.

Rnd 1: ch 4 (counts as tr). tr in ring. *ch 5. 2 tr in ring. Repeat from * 4 times. ch 5, and join with sl st in top of initial ch 4.

Rnd 2: ch 1 (counts as sc). *ch 3, and sc in next tr. ch 3. In middle of next ch 5 space, work: [dc, ch 5 and sl st in 5th ch from hook for picot, dc]. ch 3.** sc in tr. Repeat from * 4 times, and from * to ** once more. Join with sl st in initial ch 1.

Rnd 3: sl st in ch 3 loop, and ch 3 (counts as dc). dc in same ch 3 loop. *ch 3. In next ch 5 loop (at point), work: [sc, ch 3, sc, ch 4, sc, ch 3, sc]. ch 3.** Skip 1 ch 3 space, and work 2 dc in next ch 3 loop (halfway between points). Repeat from * 4 times, and from * to ** once more. Using color B, join with sl st in top of initial ch 3. Continue with B.

Rnd 4: ch 1 (counts as sc). [ch 3, sc] in same ch as last sl st. *ch 6, and sl st in 6th ch from hook, to form loop. [sc, ch 3, sc] in next dc. ch 3. Skip ch 3 space, and sl st in sc. ch 3, skip ch 3 loop, and sl st in sc. ch 4, skip ch 4 loop, and sl st in sc. ch 3, skip ch 3 loop, and sl st in sc. ch 3.** Skip ch 3 space, and [sc, ch 3, sc] in dc. Repeat from * 4 times, and from * to ** once more. Join with sl st in initial ch 1.

Rnd 5: sl st in ch 3 loop, and ch 3 (counts as dc). *In next ch 6 loop, work: [sc, ch 3, sc, ch 4, sc, ch 3, sc]. dc in next ch 3 loop. ch 3. Skip: [sc, ch 3 space, sl st, ch 3 space]. sl st in sl st. ch 5, skip ch 4 space, and sl st in sl st. ch 3.** Skip: [ch 3 space, sl st, ch 3 space, sc]. dc in ch 3 loop. Repeat from * 4 times, and from * to ** once more. Join with sl st in top of initial ch 3.

Note: If desired, use crochet hook to pull the loops at the points of Rnd 3 forward, so that they are more pronounced.

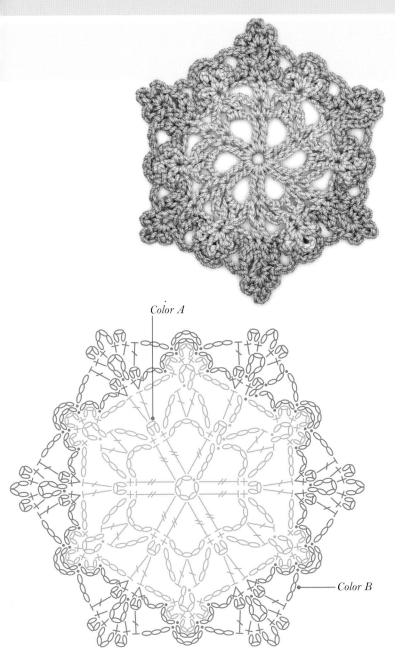

Color A

Color B

59 Water Lily

Finished diameter: 2¼ in (57 mm)

Thread required: 11 yds (10.1 m)

Foundation ring: ch 8, and join with sl st in first ch.

Rnd 1: ch 1 (counts as sc). 15 sc in ring. Join with sl st in initial ch 1.

Rnd 2: *ch 5. 2 tr in 1 sc. ch 5.** sl st in 1 sc. Repeat from * 6 times, and from * to ** once more. Join with sl st in sl st.

Rnd 3: *[3 sc, hdc] in ch 5 space. [dc, tr] in front strand only of 1 tr. [tr, dc] in front strand only of next tr. [hdc, 3 sc] in ch 5 space. sl st in sl st. Repeat from * 7 times.

Rnd 4: ch 3. *sc in the back strands only of the next 2 tr of Rnd 2 (in the middle of the next petal's back). ch 5. Repeat from * 7 times. Join with sl st in initial sc.

Rnd 5: ch 1 (counts as sc). sc in sc. *[4 dc, ch 2, 4 dc] in ch 5 space.** sc in 2 sc. Repeat from * 6 times, and from * to ** once more. Join with sl st in initial ch 1. Fasten off; weave in ends.

Rounds 1–3

Rounds 4–5

○ = ch   • = sl st   + = sc   ├── = hdc   ├─╱ = dc   ├─╱╱ = tr   ⊃ = work in front strand of stitch below   ⊂ = work in back strand of stitch below

60 Lemon Tree

Finished height: 2⅝ in (67 mm)
Thread required: color A, 6 yds (5.5 m); color B, 3 yds (2.7 m)

Right Trunk: Using color A, ch 12.
Branch 1: ch 8. *ch 5, and sl st in 2nd and 1st ch of ch 5, to form fruit stem. ch 6, and sl st in 4th ch from hook, to form loop. Bypass stem (pass thread under stem) and work the following stitches into loop: [3 sc, hdc, ch 3, hdc, 3 sc]. sl st in same ch as last sl st (at base of loop), and in next 2 ch.** ch 7, and sl st in 4th ch from hook, to form loop. Bypass stem (pass thread under stem) and work the following stitches into loop: [3 sc, hdc, ch 3, hdc, 3 sc]. sl st in same ch as last sl st (at base of loop), and in next 3 ch. Skipping the bases of the opposite leaf and fruit stems, sl st in next 2 empty ch. Repeat from * to **. sc in next 6 empty ch.
Branches 2 and 3: Repeat Branch 1 once for each of next two branches.
Left Trunk: dc in 1st ch of Branch 2, and in 1st ch of Branch 1. dc in next 2 ch. tr in 5 ch, and dtr in 2 ch. ch 3. Fasten off color A.
Fruit: Using color B, work 8 hdc in the end of the 1st fruit stem of Branch 1. Join with sl st in initial hdc. Fasten off. Repeat in each of the 5 remaining fruit stems. Weave in all ends.

Color A

Color B

○ = ch • = sl st ├── = hdc ├─✕ = dc ├─⫽⫽ = tr ├──⫽⫽⫽ = dtr

61 Grapevine

Finished length: 3⅜ in (86 mm)

Thread required: color A, 5 yds (4.6 m); color B, 3 yds (2.7 m)

Vine

Using color A, ch 20. ch 5, to make leaf stem. Make Leaf, as below. Reach hook under leaf, in order to sl st in 5th ch of ch 5 stem. Working back down stem, sl st in 4 ch. ch 14, to make grape stem. [dc, ch 5, sl st] in 9th ch of ch 14. Continuing down chain, sl st in next 8 ch. Skip base of leaf stem, and sc in the remaining 20 ch. Fasten off color A.

Leaf

Foundation ring: ch 6, and join with sl st in first ch.
Rnd 1: ch 5. 6 tr in ring. ch 3. 6 tr in ring. ch 5. sl st in ring.
Rnd 2: 5 sc in ch 5 space. hdc in 1 tr. 3 dc in 1 tr.

3 tr in 1 tr. ch 2. [hdc, sc] in 1 tr. hdc in 1 tr. [dc, tr] in 1 tr. [tr, dtr, ch 4, dtr, tr] in ch 3 space. [tr, dc] in 1 tr. hdc in 1 tr. [sc, hdc] in 1 tr. ch 2. 3 tr in 1 tr. 3 dc in 1 tr. hdc in 1 tr. 5 sc in ch 5 space. Join with sl st in sl st.

Grapes

Row 1: Using color B, sl st in 12th ch of last ch 14 (the grape stem). ch 3 (counts as dc). 4 dc in same ch. ch 1. Skip 2 ch, and 5 dc in dc. ch 1. Skip 2 ch, and 5 dc in 1 ch. Turn.
Row 2: ch 3. Skip 1 dc. *3-dc decrease in 3 dc. ch 3.** sl st in 1 dc. ch 2. Skip ch 1 space, and sl st in dc. ch 3. Repeat from * once, and from * to ** once more. sl st in 1 ch. Turn.

Row 3: ch 6. Pass chain behind the next grape, and sl st in next ch 2 point. ch 3 (counts as dc). 4 dc in same ch 2 point. ch 1. Skip next grape (passing chain behind it), and 5 dc in next ch 2 point. Turn.
Row 4: ch 3. Skip 1 dc. *3-dc decrease in 3 dc. ch 3.** sl st in 1 dc. ch 2. Skip ch 1 space, and sl st in dc. ch 3. Repeat from * to ** once. sl st in 1 ch. Turn.
Row 5: ch 6. Run chain behind next grape, and sl st in ch 2 point. ch 3 (counts as dc). 4 dc in same ch 2 point. Turn.
Row 6: ch 3. Skip 1 dc. 3-dc decrease in 3 dc. ch 3, and sl st in 1 ch. Fasten off; weave in ends.

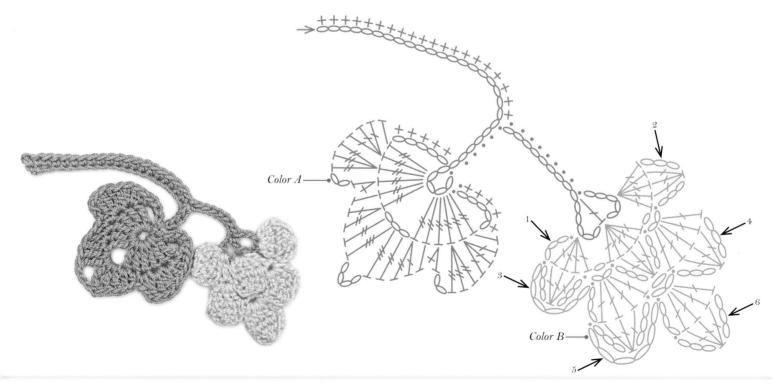

Color A

Color B

○ = ch • = sl st + = sc ├── = hdc ├─┤ = dc ├──┤ = tr ├───┤ = dtr ⇒ = beginning of vine

62 Apple Basket

Finished height: 2³/₄ in (70 mm)

Thread required: color A, 10 yd (9.1 m); color B, 2 yd (1.8 m)

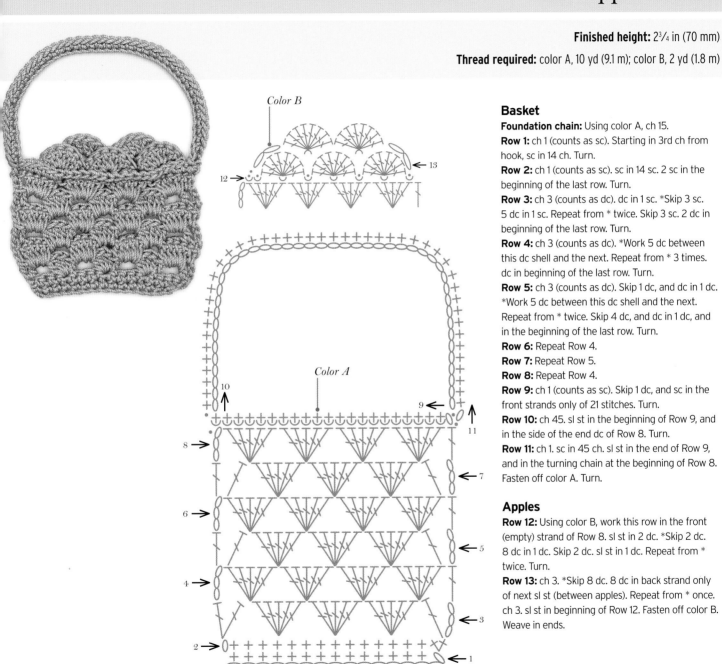

Color B

Color A

Basket

Foundation chain: Using color A, ch 15.

Row 1: ch 1 (counts as sc). Starting in 3rd ch from hook, sc in 14 ch. Turn.

Row 2: ch 1 (counts as sc). sc in 14 sc. 2 sc in the beginning of the last row. Turn.

Row 3: ch 3 (counts as dc). dc in 1 sc. *Skip 3 sc. 5 dc in 1 sc. Repeat from * twice. Skip 3 sc. 2 dc in beginning of the last row. Turn.

Row 4: ch 3 (counts as dc). *Work 5 dc between this dc shell and the next. Repeat from * 3 times. dc in beginning of the last row. Turn.

Row 5: ch 3 (counts as dc). Skip 1 dc, and dc in 1 dc. *Work 5 dc between this dc shell and the next. Repeat from * twice. Skip 4 dc, and dc in 1 dc, and in the beginning of the last row. Turn.

Row 6: Repeat Row 4.

Row 7: Repeat Row 5.

Row 8: Repeat Row 4.

Row 9: ch 1 (counts as sc). Skip 1 dc, and sc in the front strands only of 21 stitches. Turn.

Row 10: ch 45. sl st in the beginning of Row 9, and in the side of the end dc of Row 8. Turn.

Row 11: ch 1. sc in 45 ch. sl st in the end of Row 9, and in the turning chain at the beginning of Row 8. Fasten off color A. Turn.

Apples

Row 12: Using color B, work this row in the front (empty) strand of Row 8. sl st in 2 dc. *Skip 2 dc. 8 dc in 1 dc. Skip 2 dc. sl st in 1 dc. Repeat from * twice. Turn.

Row 13: ch 3. *Skip 8 dc. 8 dc in back strand only of next sl st (between apples). Repeat from * once. ch 3. sl st in beginning of Row 12. Fasten off color B. Weave in ends.

◯ = ch   •́ = sl st   + = sc   ├──┤ = hdc   ├─⤢ = dc   ⊂ = work in back strand of stitch below   ⊃ = work in front strand of stitch below

63 Pumpkin

Finished height: 2⅝ in (67 mm)

Thread required: color A, 11 yds (10.1m); color B, 1 yd (0.9 m)

Foundation ring: Using color A, ch 4, and join with sl st in first ch.

Rnd 1: ch 1 (counts as sc). 7 sc in ring. Join with sl st in initial ch 1.

Rnd 2: ch 5 (counts as dtr). 3 dtr in same ch as last sl st. *3 tr in 1 sc, dc in 1 sc, and 3 tr in 1 sc.** 4 dtr in 1 sc. Repeat from * to ** once. Join with sl st in top of initial ch 5.

Rnd 3: ch 5 (counts as dtr). dtr in same ch as last sl st. 2 dtr in each of 3 dtr. *2 tr in each of 3 tr. 3 dc in dc. 2 tr in each of 3 tr.** 2 dtr in each of 4 dtr. Repeat from * to **. Join with sl st in top of initial ch 5.

Rnd 4: ch 2 (counts as hdc). ch 3. Skip 1 dtr, and sc in 4 dtr. ch 3. Skip 1 dtr, and hdc in 1 dtr. *ch 4. Skip 1 stitch, and dc in 1 stitch.** Repeat from * to ** 6 times. ch 4. Skip 3 stitches. sc in 4 dtr. ch 4. Skip 3 stitches, and dc in 1 tr. Repeat from * to ** 6 times. ch 4, and join with sl st in top of initial ch 2.

Rnd 5: sl st in ch 3 space, and ch 1 (counts as sc). 2 sc in same ch 3 space. sl st in 4 sc. 3 sc in ch 3 space. 5 dc in each of 3 ch 4 spaces. 4 dc in each of 3 ch 4 spaces. 3 sc in each of 2 ch 4 spaces. sl st in 4 sc. 3 sc in each of 2 ch 4 spaces, 4 dc in each of 3 ch 4 spaces, and 5 dc in each of 3 ch 4 spaces. sl st in initial ch 1, and in 1 sc.

Stem: Using color B, [sl st, ch 5, dtr] in next sc. Skip 1 sl st. dtr in 2 sl st. Skip 1 sl st. [dtr, ch 5, sl st] in sc. Fasten off; weave in ends.

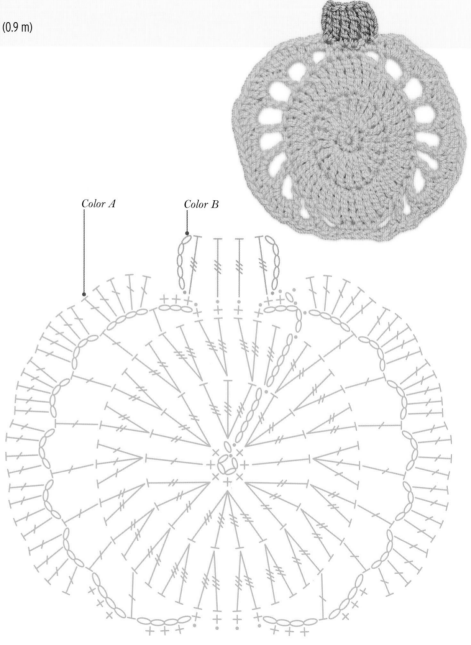

Color A   *Color B*

○ = ch • = sl st + = sc ├─╱── = dc ├─╫── = tr ├─╫╫── = dtr

64 Angel

Finished height: 2³⁄₈ in (60 mm)
Thread required: 8 yds (7.3 m)

Foundation ring: ch 5, and join with sl st in first ch.
Rnd 1: ch 1 (counts as sc). 8 sc in ring. Join with sl st in initial ch 1.
Rnd 2: In next sc, work: [sl st, ch 4, 4-tr cluster, ch 4, sl st]. sl st in 1 sc. *[sc, ch 3, tr] in 1 sc. [tr, ch 3, sc] in 1 sc.** [sc, ch 3, 2 tr] in 1 sc. [2 tr, ch 3, sc] in 1 sc. Repeat from * to **. Join with sl st in sl st.
Rnd 3: ch 16. Skip: [sl st, ch 4 space, tr cluster, ch 4 space, 1 sl st]. sl st in next sl st, and in sc. ch 4. Skip ch 3 space, and 3 dc in 1 tr. [dc, tr, dtr] in 1 tr. ch 7. sl st in ch 3 space. ch 2. Skip 1 sc, and sl st in 1 sc. ch 7. Skip ch 3 space, and dc in tr. [ch 3, dc] in each of 3 tr. ch 7. Skip ch 3 space, and sl st in 1 sc. ch 2. Skip sc, and sl st in ch 3 space. ch 7. [dtr, tr, dc] in 1 tr. 3 dc in 1 tr. ch 4. Skip ch 3 space, and sl st in sc. Join with sl st in sl st.
Rnd 4: 16 sc in ch 16 space. Skip 1 sl st, and sl st in 1 sl st. 4 sc in ch 4 space. 3 dc in 1 dc. dc in 3 dc, and in 1 tr. [dc, 2 tr, dtr, ch 7, sc] in dtr. 4 sc in ch 7 space. sl st in ch 2 space, and in sl st. ch 4. [sl st, ch 8, tr] in ch 7 space. [tr, ch 4, tr] in each of next 3 ch 3 spaces. [tr, ch 8, sl st] in ch 7 space. ch 4. sl st in sl st, and in ch 2 space. 4 sc in ch 7 space. [sc, ch 7, dtr, 2 tr, dc] in dtr. dc in tr, and in 3 dc. 3 dc in dc. 4 sc in ch 4 space. Join with sl st in sl st. Fasten off; weave in ends.

○ = ch   • = sl st   + = sc   ⊢—⊣ = dc   ⊢—⫝⊣ = tr   ⊢—⫴⊣ = dtr

65 Snowflake Doily

Finished diameter: 5⁷/₈ in (149 mm)

Thread required: 32 yds (29.3 m)

Foundation ring: ch 6 and join with sl st in first ch.
Rnd 1: ch 1 (counts as sc). 11 sc in ring. Join with sl st in initial ch 1.
Rnd 2: ch 4 (counts as tr). tr in 1 sc. *ch 6. tr in 2 sc. Repeat from * 4 times. ch 6, and join with sl st in top of initial ch 4.
Rnd 3: ch 1 (counts as sc). *ch 4, and sc in next tr. ch 6. tr in middle of ch 6 space. ch 6.** sc in tr. Repeat from * 4 times, and from * to ** once more. Join with sl st in initial ch 1.
Rnd 4: sl st in 1 ch, and in ch 4 loop. ch 1 (counts as sc). *ch 4. Skip sc, and skip ch 4 space. In tr, work: [2 dc, ch 2, 2 dc, ch 5, 2 dc, ch 2, 2 dc]. ch 4. Skip ch 4 space, and skip sc.** sc in ch 4 loop. Repeat from * 4 times, and from * to ** once more. Join with sl st in initial ch 1.
Rnd 5: sl st in 1 ch, and in ch 4 space. ch 1 (counts as sc). *ch 3, skip 2 dc, and [sc, ch 4, sc] in ch 2 point. ch 3, skip 2 dc, and [sc, ch 4, sc] in ch 5 point. ch 3, skip 2 dc, and [sc, ch 4, sc] in ch 2 point. ch 3, and sc in 1 ch 4 space. ch 2.** sc in next ch 4 space. Repeat from * 4 times, and from * to ** once. Join with sl st in initial ch 1.
Rnd 6: sl st in 3 ch, in sc, in 1 ch, and in ch 4 loop. ch 3 (counts as dc). *ch 4. Skip ch 3 space. In next ch 4 loop, work: [2 dc, ch 2, 2 dc, ch 5, 2 dc, ch 2, 2 dc]. ch 4. Skip ch 3 space, and dc in ch 4 loop. ch 2. Skip ch 3 space, and tr in ch 2 space. ch 2.** Skip ch 3 space, and dc in ch 4 loop. Repeat from * 4 times, and from * to ** once more. Join with sl st in top of initial ch 3.
Rnd 7: sl st in 2 ch, and in ch 4 space. ch 1 (counts as sc). *ch 3. Skip 2 dc. [sc, dc, ch 3, dc, sc] in ch 2 point. ch 2. Skip 2 dc. [sc, dc, ch 5, dc, sc] in ch 5 point. ch 2. Skip 2 dc. [sc, dc, ch 3, dc, sc] in ch 2 point. Skip 2 dc.** [ch 3, sc] in ch 4 space, in each of 2 ch 2 spaces, and in ch 4 space, skipping the stitches between them. Repeat from * 4 times, and

from * to ** once more. [ch 3, sc] in ch 4 space, and in each of 2 ch 2 spaces. ch 3, and join with sl st in initial ch 1.
Rnd 8: sl st in 1 ch, and in ch 3 space. ch 3 (counts as dc). *ch 2. In next ch 3 point, work: [2 sc, ch 4, sc, ch 6, sc, ch 4, 2 sc]. ch 2. In next ch 5 point, work: [2 sc, ch 4, sc, ch 6, sc, ch 8, sc, ch 6, sc, ch 4, 2 sc]. ch 2. In next ch 3 point, work: [2 sc, ch 4, sc, ch 6, sc, ch 4, 2 sc]. ch 2. dc in next ch 3 space. Skip 1 ch 3 space, and in next ch 3 space, work: [dc, ch 7 and sl st in 5th ch from hook, ch 2, dc].** Skip 1 ch 3 space, and dc in next ch 3 space. Repeat from * 4 times, and from * to ** once more. Join with sl st in top of initial ch 3. Fasten off; weave in ends.

○ = ch • = sl st + = sc ⊢—— = dc ⊢—— = tr

66 Christmas Tree

Finished height: 2¾ in (70 mm)
Thread required: 9 yds (8.2 m)
Other materials: 11 round beads

Note: Before beginning, string all 11 beads onto the thread you'll be using. They will "ride" on the thread ahead of your stitches, and you'll slide them into place as the pattern calls for them.

Row 1: ch 6. 4 tr in 1st ch of ch 6. Turn.
Row 2: ch 5 (counts as lengthened tr). tr in 1 tr. 2tr in 1 tr. tr in 1 tr. Place 1 bead after the stitch, and ch 1 to anchor it. sl st in top of last tr made. 2 tr in tr, and in 1 ch. Turn.
Row 3: ch 1. Skip 1 tr, and sl st in 2 tr. ch 5 (counts as lengthened tr). 2 tr in same tr as last sl st. ch 2. Skip: [tr, sl st, ch 1, bead]. 3 tr in 1 tr. ch 2. Skip 1 tr, and 3 tr in 1 tr. Turn.
Row 4: ch 5 (counts as lengthened tr). tr in 2 tr. 2 tr in 1 tr. *ch 2. Place 1 bead after the stitch, and ch 1 to anchor it. sc in ch 2 space. ch 2. 2 tr in 1 tr. tr in 1 tr.** 2 tr in 1 tr. Repeat from * to **. 2 tr in 1 ch. Turn.
Row 5: ch 1. Skip 1 tr, and sl st in 2 tr. ch 5 (counts as lengthened tr). 2 tr in same tr as last sl st. ch 2. Skip: [2 tr, ch 2 space, sc, ch 1, bead, ch 2 space]. 3 tr in 1 tr. ch 2. Skip 3 tr. 3 tr in 1 tr. ch 2. Skip: [ch 2 space, sc, ch 1, bead, ch 2 space, 2 tr]. 3 tr in 1 tr. Turn.
Row 6: ch 5 (counts as lengthened tr). tr in 2 tr. 2 tr in 1 tr. *ch 2. Place 1 bead after the stitch, and ch 1 to anchor it. sc in ch 2 space. ch 2. 2 tr in 1 tr. tr in 1 tr.** 2 tr in 1 tr. Repeat from * once, and from * to ** once. 2 tr in 1 ch. Turn.
Row 7: ch 1. Skip 1 tr, and sl st in 2 tr. ch 5 (counts as lengthened tr). 2 tr in same tr as last sl st. ch 2. Skip 2 tr. *Skip: [ch 2 space, sc, ch 1, bead, ch 2 space]. 3 tr in 1 tr. ch 2. Skip 3 tr. 3 tr in 1 tr. ch 2. Repeat from * once. Skip: [ch 2 space, sc, ch 1, bead, ch 2 space, 2 tr]. 3 tr in 1 tr. Turn.
Row 8: ch 5 (counts as lengthened tr). tr in 2 tr. 2 tr in 1 tr. *ch 2. Place 1 bead after the stitch, and ch 1 to anchor it. sc in ch 2 space. ch 2. 2 tr in 1 tr. tr in 1 tr.** 2 tr in 1 tr. Repeat from * 3 times, and from * to ** once more. 2 tr in 1 ch. Fasten off; weave in ends.

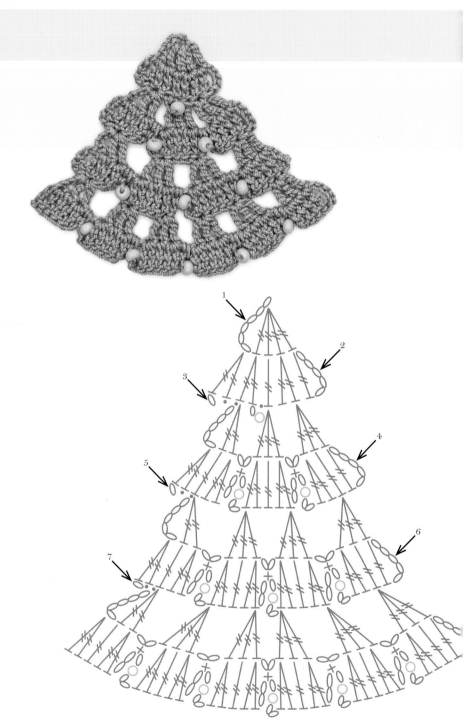

○ = ch　•= sl st　+ = sc　⊢—— = tr　⟶ = beginning of tree　○ = bead

67 Christmas Stocking

Finished height: 3⅝ in (92 mm)

Thread required: color A, 4 yds (3.7 m); color B, 5 yds (4.6 m)

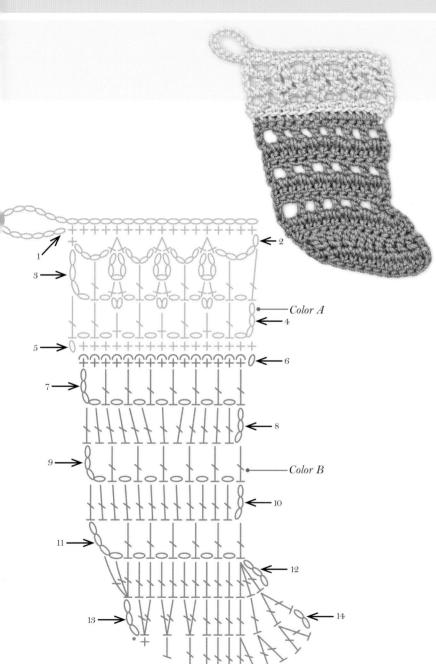

Foundation chain: Using color A, ch 30.

Row 1: sc in 14th ch from hook, and in next 16 ch. Turn.

Row 2: ch 5 (counts as sc + ch 4). Skip 4 sc. *[sc, ch 5, sc] in 1 sc. ch 4. Skip 3 sc. Repeat from * twice. sc in 1 sc. Turn.

Row 3: ch 4 (counts as dc + ch 1). *dc in ch 4 space. ch 1.** [sc, ch 2, sc] in ch 5 loop. ch 1. Repeat from * twice, and from * to ** once more. dc in beginning of Row 2. Turn.

Row 4: ch 4 (counts as dc + ch 1). Skip ch 1 space, and dc in dc. *ch 1. Skip ch 1 space, and skip sc. sc in ch 2 point. ch 1. Skip sc, and skip ch 1 space. dc in dc. Repeat from * twice. ch 1, skip ch 1 space, and dc in beginning of Row 3. Turn.

Row 5: ch 1 (counts as sc). Skip dc. sc in each ch 1 space and in each stitch, to end (total 16 stitches). Turn.

Row 6: Using color B, ch 1. Continue with B. Skip 1 sc, and sc in front strand only of 15 stitches. Turn.

Row 7: ch 4 (counts as dc + ch 1). Skip 2 sc, and dc in 1 sc. [ch 1, skip 1 stitch, and dc in 1 stitch] 6 times. Turn.

Row 8: ch 3 (counts as dc). Skip dc. dc in next 5 ch 1 spaces and dc. [Skip 1 dc, and dc in ch 1 space] twice. dc in next 4 ch 1 spaces and dc. dc in beginning of Row 7. Turn.

Row 9: ch 4 (counts as dc + ch 1). Skip 2 dc, and dc in 1 dc. [ch 1, skip 1 stitch, and dc in 1 stitch] 5 times. Turn.

Row 10: ch 3 (counts as dc). Skip dc. dc in each ch 1 space, and in each stitch to end (total 12 stitches). Turn.

Row 11: ch 4 (counts as dc + ch 1). Skip 3 dc, and dc in 1 dc. [ch 1, skip 1 stitch, and dc in 1 stitch] 4 times. ch 1, and dc in beginning of Row 10. Turn.

Row 12: ch 3. 3 dc in 1 dc. dc in next 9 ch 1 spaces and stitches. Work 3-dc decrease with 1 dc in dc, 1 dc in ch 1 space, and 1 dc in ch. Turn.

Row 13: ch 3. Skip dc decrease. [2-dc decrease in 2 dc] 3 times. dc in 5 dc. 2 dc in 1 dc. Turn.

Row 14: ch 2. Skip 1 dc. 2 dc in each of 3 dc. dc in 4 stitches, hdc in 1 dc decrease, sc in 1 dc decrease, and sl st in 1 ch. Fasten off; weave in ends.

Color A

Color B

○ = ch   • = sl st   + = sc   ├── = hdc   ├─/ = dc   ⊃ = work in front strand of stitch below

68 Menorah

Finished height: 2¾ in (70 mm)

Thread required: color A, 7 yds (6.4 m); color B, 3 yds (2.7 m)

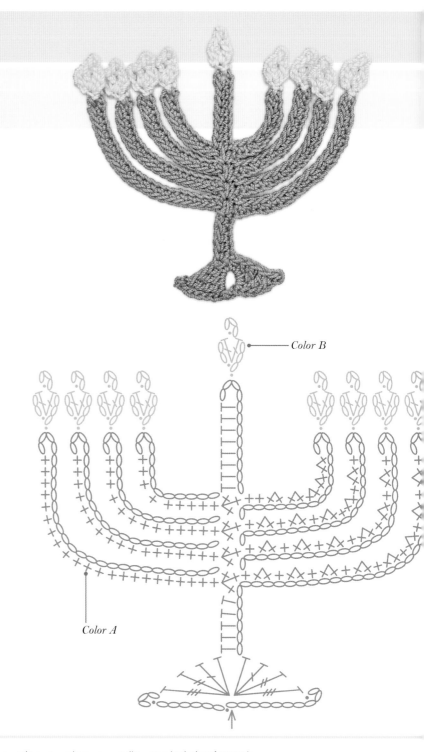

Color B

Color A

Note: For purposes of this pattern, all candles except the Shamash candle are numbered in the order that they're crocheted, from right to left.

Right Base: Using color A, ch 10. sl st in 3rd ch from hook to form picot. [dtr, tr, dc, hdc] in 1st ch of ch 10. ch 6.

Candle 1: ch 29. sc in 5th ch from hook. *Continuing down the chain, 2-sc decrease in 2 ch. sc in 1 ch. Repeat from * 7 times.

Candle 2: ch 24. sc in 5th ch from hook. *Continuing down the chain, 2-sc decrease in 2 ch. sc in 1 ch. Repeat from * 5 times.

Candle 3: ch 21. sc in 5th ch from hook. *Continuing down the chain, 2-sc decrease in 2 ch. sc in 1 ch. Repeat from * 4 times.

Candle 4: ch 17. Starting in 5th ch from hook, work 5 2-sc decreases in a total of 10 ch. sc in 2 ch.

Shamash Candle: ch 12. Starting in 5th ch from hook, hdc in 8 ch.

Candle 5: ch 13. Starting in 5th ch from hook, sc in 9 ch. Work 3-sc decrease with 1 sc in side of last hdc made, 1 sc in side of opposite sc (at bottom of Candle 4), and 1 sc in nearest empty ch (below Candle 4).

Candle 6: ch 17. Starting in 5th ch from hook, sc in 13 ch. Work 3-sc decrease with 1 sc in side of last sc decrease made (at bottom of Candle 5), 1 sc in side of opposite sc (at bottom of Candle 3), and 1 sc in nearest empty ch (below Candle 3).

Candle 7: ch 21. Starting in 5th ch from hook, sc in 17 ch. Work 3-sc decrease with 1 sc in side of last sc decrease made (at bottom of Candle 6), 1 sc in side of opposite sc (at bottom of Candle 2), and 1 sc in nearest empty ch (below Candle 2).

Candle 8: ch 26. Starting in 5th ch from hook, sc in 22 ch. Work 3-sc decrease with 1 sc in side of last sc decrease made (at bottom of Candle 7), 1 sc in side of opposite sc (at bottom of Candle 1), and 1 sc in nearest empty ch (below Candle 1).

Left Base: hdc in 5 ch. In 1st ch of Right base, work: [hdc, dc, tr, dtr, ch 3 and sl st in 3rd ch from hook for picot, ch 6, sl st]. Fasten off color A.

Flames: Using color B, sl st in ch 4 point at tip of Candle 1. ch 3. In 1st ch of ch 3, work: [dc, ch 3 and sl st in 3rd ch from hook for picot, dc, ch 2, sl st]. Fasten off. Repeat flame in each candle, and weave in ends.

○ = ch   • = sl st   + = sc   ⊢— = hdc   ⊢/— = dc   ⊢//— = tr   ⊢///— = dtr   ⟶ = beginning of menorah

69 Hot Air Balloon

Finished height: 2³⁄₄ in (70 mm)

Thread required: 6 yds (5.5 m)

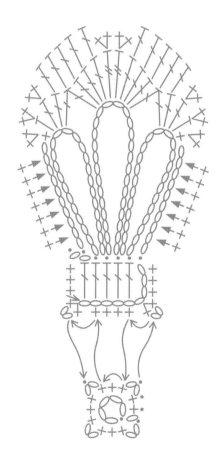

Balloon

Foundation chain: ch 6.

Row 1: ch 3 (counts as dc). Beginning in 5th ch from hook, dc in 5 ch. Turn.

Row 2: ch 1. Skip 1 dc, and sl st in 1 dc. ch 24, and sl st in 1 dc for loop. ch 28, and sl st in next dc. ch 24, and sl st in next dc. sl st in 1 ch. Turn.

Row 3: ch 10. [sc, hdc, 2 dc] in top of ch 24 loop. Work 1 2-dc decrease with the first dc in this loop, and the second in the ch 28 loop. [3 dc, 2 tr, 3 dc] in same ch 28 loop. Work 1 2-dc decrease with the first dc in this loop, and the second in the next ch 24 loop. [2 dc, hdc, sc] in same ch 24 loop. ch 10. Skip sl st, and sl st in 1 ch. Do not turn.

Border: ch 1 (counts as sc). 2 sc down side of next dc. [sc, ch 2, sc] in 1 ch. sc in 4 ch. [sc, ch 2, sc] in 1 ch. sc in 3 ch. 7 sc over ch 10, and into the ch 24 loop beneath it. 2 sc in sc, in hdc, and in 1 dc. dc in dc, in dc decrease, and in 3 dc. 2 sc in each of 2 tr. dc in 3 dc, in dc decrease, and in 1 dc. 2 sc in dc, in hdc, and in sc. 7 sc over ch 10, and into the ch 24 loop beneath it. Join with sl st in initial ch 1. Fasten off.

Gondola

Foundation ring: ch 5, and join with sl st in first ch.

Rnd 1: ch 1 (counts as sc). 2 sc in ring. *ch 2. 3 sc in ring. Repeat from * twice. ch 2, and join with sl st in initial ch 1. sl st in 2 sc, and in ch 2 point. Fasten off, leaving thread end approximately 6 in (152 mm) long.

Connecting Ropes

Using hook, feed long thread end from the Gondola through the ch 2 point at the lower right corner of the Balloon. (Leave about ¹⁄₂ in [13 mm] of thread between top of Gondola and bottom of Balloon.) Working left, across the bottom of Balloon, skip 1 sc, and pull thread through the top of next sc. Then connect to next sc of Gondola (maintaining distance between Balloon and Gondola). Skip 1 sc of Gondola, and pull thread through next (leftmost) sc. Continuing across the bottom of the balloon, skip 2 sc and pull thread through next sc. Then skip 1 sc, and pull thread through ch 2 point at Balloon's lower left corner. Pull thread through upper left corner of Gondola, anchor with sl st in this point, and fasten off. Weave in ends.

70 Kite

Finished width: 4¼ in (108 mm)

Thread required: color A, 4 yds (3.7 m); color B, 3 yds (2.7 m)

Crosspiece: Using color A, ch 15. Beginning in 3rd ch from hook, and working back down chain, sc in 5 ch. {1st arm complete.} ch 9. Beginning in 3rd ch from hook and working back down chain, dc in 7 ch. ch 7. Beginning in 3rd ch from hook and working back down chain, sc in 4 ch. 2-sc decrease in 1 ch, and in side of nearest sc of the 1st arm. sc in next 8 ch (the remainder of the initial ch 15).

Fabric: Using color B, sl st in same ch as last sc. Continuing around Crosspiece with color B, sc in 1 ch, hdc in 1 ch, and dc in 1 ch. 4-tr decrease in 4 ch. Skip 1 ch, then tr in 1 ch, dc in 1 ch, hdc in 1 ch, sc in 1 ch, and sl st in 2 ch. sc in 1 sc, hdc in 1 sc, dc in 1 sc, and tr in 1 sc. Skip 1 sc. 4-tr decrease in 4 ch, dc in 1 ch, hdc in 1 ch, sc in 1 ch, and sl st in 2 ch. sc in 1 sc, hdc in 1 sc, and dc in 1 sc. 4-tr decrease in 4 sc. Skip 1 ch. tr in 1 ch, dc in 1 ch, hdc in 1 ch, and sc in 1 ch. sl st in 2 ch. sc in 1 sc, hdc in 1 sc, dc in 1 sc, and tr in 1 sc. Skip sc decrease. 4-tr decrease in 4 sc. dc in 1 sc, hdc in 1 sc, and sc in 1 sc. Using color A, sl st in sc. Continue with A.

Border: sl st in next sl st, and ch 1 (counts as sc). sc in same sl st. *sc in 8 stitches. 2 sc in 1 sl st.** ch 3. 2 sc in next sl st. Repeat from * twice, and from * to ** once more.

Tail: *ch 9. [dc, ch 3, sl st] in 6th ch of ch 9. Repeat from * twice. ch 8. Beginning in 3rd ch from hook, sl st in 6 ch. **In next ch (at base of next dc/sl st grouping), work: [sl st, ch 3, dc, ch 3, sl st]. sl st in 5 ch. Repeat from ** twice. sl st in initial ch 1 of Border. Fasten off; weave in ends.

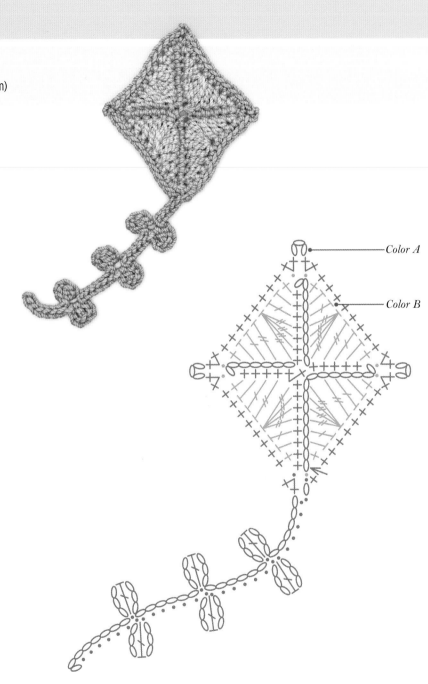

Color A

Color B

○ = ch • = sl st + = sc ├── = hdc ├─< = dc ├─⧣ = tr ├─⧣⧣ = dtr ⟶ = beginning of kite

71 Angel Fish

Finished length: 2⅝ in (67 mm)

Thread required: 6 yds (5.5 m)

Row 1: ch 7. dc in 1st ch of ch 7. Turn.
Row 2: ch 3 (counts as dc). ch 3, and dc in ch 7 space. ch 3, and dc in 4th ch of ch 7 made in Row 1. Turn.
Row 3: ch 3 (counts as dc). ch 2. Skip ch 3 space, and 7 tr in dc. ch 2. Skip 3 ch, and dc in 1 ch. Turn.
Row 4: ch 3 (counts as dc). dc in 1 dc. ch 3. Skip ch 2 space, and sc in 1 tr. [ch 2, sc] in each of 6 tr. ch 3. Skip 2 ch. 3 dc in 1 ch. Turn.
Row 5: ch 3 (counts as dc). dc in 2 dc. ch 2, and sl st in dc. ch 6. Skip ch 3 space, and skip sc. sc in ch 2 point. [ch 2, sc] in each of 5 ch 2 points. ch 3. Skip sc, and skip ch 3 space. dc in dc, and in 1 ch. Turn.
Row 6: ch 3 (counts as dc). Skip 1 dc, and 2 dc in 1 dc. ch 3. Skip ch 3 space, and skip sc. sc in ch 2 point. [ch 2, sc] in each of 4 ch 2 points. ch 3. Skip sc, and skip 3 ch. 2 dc in 1 ch. Turn.
Row 7: ch 3 (counts as dc). Skip 1 dc, and 2 dc in 1 dc. ch 3. Skip ch 3 space, and skip sc. sc in ch 2 point. [ch 2, sc] in each of 3 ch 2 points. ch 3. Skip sc, and skip ch 3 space. 2 dc in 1 dc. dc in dc, and in 1 ch. Turn.
Row 8: ch 6, and sl st in 3rd ch from hook for picot. tr in 2 dc. dc in 1 dc, and 2 dc in 1 dc. ch 3. Skip ch 3 space, and skip sc. sc in ch 2 point. [ch 2, sc] in each of 2 ch 2 points. ch 3. Skip sc, and skip ch 3 space. 2 dc in 1 dc. Skip 1 dc, and dc in 1 dc. Turn.
Row 9: ch 2. Skip 2 dc, and 2 dc in 1 dc. ch 3. Skip ch 3 space, and skip sc. sc in ch 2 point. [ch 2, sc] in next ch 2 point. ch 3. Skip sc, and skip ch 3 space. dc in 1 dc. Turn.
Row 10: ch 6 (counts as dc + ch 3). Skip ch 3 space, and skip sc. sc in ch 2 point. ch 3. Skip sc, and skip ch 3 space. dc in 1 dc. Turn.
Row 11: ch 1 (counts as sc). ch 2. Skip ch 3 space, and dc in sc. ch 2. Skip 3 ch, and sc in 1 ch. Turn.
Row 12: ch 1 (counts as sc). Skip sc. 2 sc in ch 2 space, sc in dc, 2 sc in ch 2 space, and sc in ch. Turn.
Row 13: ch 3 (counts as dc). dc in 4 sc, tr in 2 sc, and 2 tr in ch. Fasten off; weave in ends.

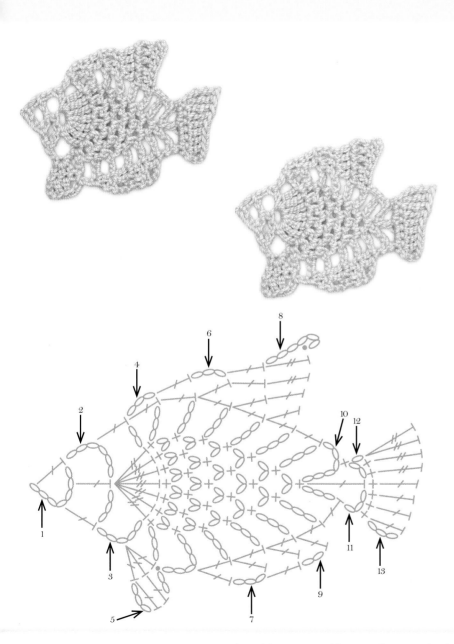

○ = ch • = sl st + = sc ┝── = hdc ┝╌─ = dc ┝╪── = tr ⇒ = beginning of fish

72 Songbird

Finished width: 2⁷/₈ in (73 mm)

Thread required: 7 yds (6.4 m)

Note: This pattern is crocheted in rounds around a foundation chain.

Foundation chain: ch 18.
Rnd 1: Starting in 3rd ch from hook, sc in 15 ch.
5 sc in the end ch. Working down the other side
of the chain, sc in 16 ch.
Rnd 2: ch 9, and sl st in 9th ch from hook, to
form loop. ch 10, and sl st in 10th ch from hook,
to form loop. Skip the ch 2 point, and sc in next
9 sc. *ch 14, and sc in top of the last sc made, to
form loop. Repeat from * 3 times. ch 18, and sc in
top of the last sc made, to form loop. sc down the
sides of the next 3 sc (at the bottoms of the ch 14
loops). Back on the bird's body, sc in 6 sc. 2 sc in
each of 5 sc. Skip 1 sc, sl st in 1 sc, and skip 1 sc. sc in
1 sc, hdc in 1 sc, 2 dc in 1 sc, and dc in 1 sc. ch 15, and
sl st in 1st ch of ch 15, to form loop. ch 12, and sl st in
1st ch of last ch 15. Back on bird's body, dc in same
sc as last dc. 2 dc in 1 sc, dc in 1 sc, hdc in 2 sc, and
sc in 1 sc. Skip 1 sc, and sl st in 3 sc.
Rnd 3: ch 6, and sc in ch 9 loop. ch 1, and sc in
ch 10 loop. ch 7. Skip sl st, and sc in 5 sc. Skip 4 sc.
In 1st ch 14 loop of wing, work: [5 sc, ch 1, dc, ch 4,
sc]. In each of the next 3 ch 14 loops, work: [sc, ch 1,
dc, ch 4, sc]. In ch 18 loop, work: [3 sc, ch 1, dc, ch 4,
9 sc]. sc in 1 sc, and hdc in 2 sc. Skip 3 sc. sl st in 12
sc. ch 3, and sl st in 2nd ch from hook for picot. ch 1.
Skip next ch (1st ch of ch 3), and sl st in 6 stitches.
ch 2. In ch 15 loop, work: [3 sc, ch 4, dc, ch 1, sc].
6 sc in ch 12 loop. ch 2. Skip sl st, and skip 3 dc.
sl st in 1 dc. Fasten off; weave in ends.

○ = ch   •= sl st   + = sc   ├─ = hdc   ├─ = dc   ⟶ = beginning of bird

73 Hummingbird

Finished height: 2½ in (64 mm)
Thread required: 6 yds (5.5 m)

Note: This pattern is crocheted in rounds around a foundation chain.

Foundation chain: ch 18.
Rnd 1: Starting in 3rd ch from hook, sc in 15 ch. 5 sc in the end ch. Working down the other side of the chain, sc in 16 ch.
Rnd 2: ch 9, and sl st in 9th ch from hook to form loop. ch 8, and sl st in 8th ch from hook, to form loop. Skip the ch 2 point, and sc in next 11 sc. *ch 14, and sc in top of the last sc made to form loop. Repeat from * 3 times. ch 18, and sc in top of the last sc made to form loop. sc down the sides of the next 3 sc (at the bottoms of the ch 14 loops). Back on the bird's body, sc in 2 sc, hdc in 1 sc, and dc in 1 sc. 2 dc in each of the next 3 sc. [2 dc, tr] in 1 sc. ch 5, and sl st in 4th and 3rd ch of ch 5. ch 2. sl st in top of the last tr made. [dc, 2 hdc] in next sc. sc in 1 sc. Skip 1 sc, sl st in 1 sc, skip 1 sc, and sc in 2 sc. hdc in 6 sc. sc in 1 sc. Skip 1 sc, and sl st in 1 sc.
Rnd 3: (This partial round ends after the wing is complete.) Skip sc, and sl st in ch at the base of the next loop. [4 sc, ch 2, 2 sc] in ch 9 loop. 5 sc in ch 8 loop. sl st over next sl st and into the ch at the base of the ch 8 loop. sc in 8 sc. Skip 3 sc, and work in the ch 14 loop: [3 sc, hdc, dc, ch 2, dc, hdc]. Then [hdc, dc, ch 2, dc, hdc] in each of the next 3 ch 14 loops. In the ch 18 loop: [sc, hdc, dc, ch 2, dc, hdc, 11 sc]. sc in 3 sc, and sl st in 1 sc. Fasten off; weave in ends.

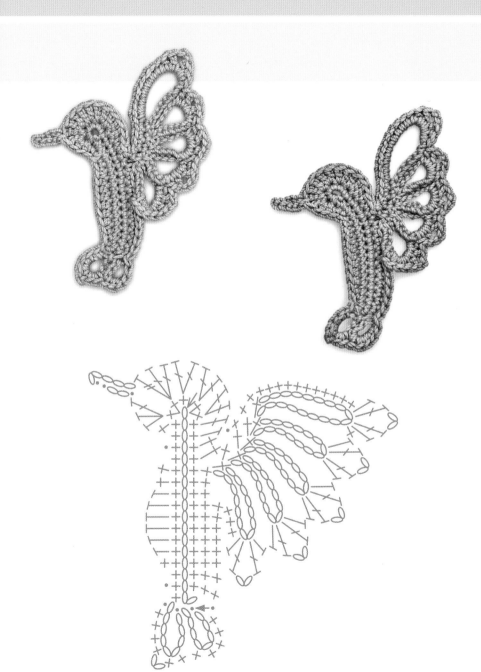

○ = ch   • = sl st   ├── = hdc   ├─✓ = dc   ├─✗ = tr   •──➤ = sl st over stitch, and into stitch below   ──➤ = beginning of bird

74 Peacock

Finished width: 2⁷/₈ in (73 mm)

Thread required: 7 yds (6.4 m)

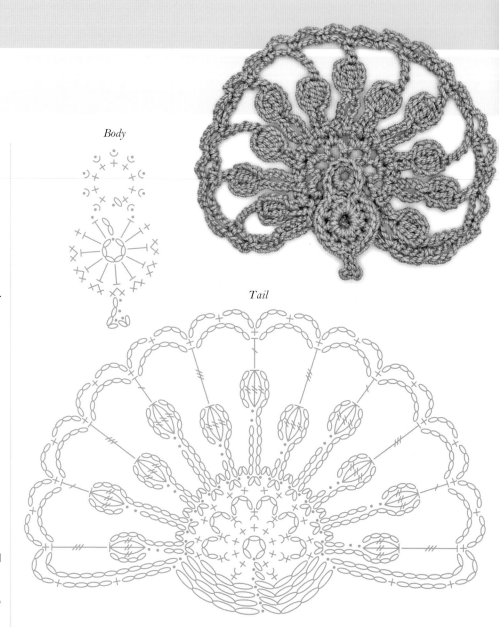

Body

Tail

Tail

Foundation ring: ch 5, and join with sl st in first ch.

Rnd 1: ch 1 (counts as sc). 9 sc in ring. Join with sl st in initial ch 1.

Rnd 2: Work this round in the back strands only of Rnd 1. ch 1 (counts as sc). sc in 2 sc. [ch 4, sc] in each of 6 sc. sc in 1 sc. Join with sl st in initial ch 1.

Rnd 3: ch 3, skip 2 sc, and [sc, ch 2, sc] in ch 4 space. [ch 2, sc] twice in each of the next 5 ch 4 spaces. ch 3. Skip 2 sc, and join with sl st in sl st.

Rnd 4: ch 4, skip ch 3 space, and sl st in ch 2 space. *ch 8. In 4th ch of ch 8, work: [3-tr cluster, ch 4, sl st]. sl st in 3rd ch of ch 8. ch 2. Skip 2 ch, and sl st in last ch 2 space worked in.** ch 2. sl st in next ch 2 space. ch 11. In 7th ch of ch 11, work: [3-tr cluster, ch 4, sl st]. sl st in 6th ch of ch 11. ch 5. Skip 5 ch, and sl st in last ch 2 space worked in. ch 2. sl st in next ch 2 space. Repeat from * 4 times, and from * to ** once more. ch 4, skip ch 3 space, and join with sl st in sl st.

Rnd 5: ch 4, skip ch 4 space, and sl st in sl st. ch 12. *dtr in top of next 3-tr cluster.** ch 7. dc in top of next 3-tr cluster. ch 7. Repeat from * 4 times, and from * to ** once more. ch 12. Skip ch 4 space, skip sl st, skip ch 2 space, and join with sl st in sl st at bottom of feather. ch 4, skip ch 4 space, and join with sl st in sl st.

Rnd 6: ch 4, skip ch 4 space, and sl st in sl st. [ch 4, sc] twice in ch 12 space. *[ch 4, sc] in dtr.** [ch 4, sc] in ch 7 space, in dc, and in ch 7 space. Repeat from * 4 times, and from * to ** once more. [ch 4, sc] twice in ch 12 space. ch 4, and sl st in sl st. ch 4, skip ch 4 space, and join with sl st in sl st. Fasten off.

Body

Foundation ring: ch 6, and join with sl st in first ch.

Rnd 1: ch 2 (counts as hdc). 11 hdc in ring. Do not join.

Rnd 2: sl st in front strand only of 1st (bottom) sc of Tail Rnd 1, and in the front strands of the next 8 sc.

Returning to Body, skip the ch 2 at the start of Rnd 1, and sl st in 1 hdc. sc in 1 hdc. 2 sc in each of 3 hdc. sc in 1 hdc. ch 4, and sl st in 2nd ch from hook for picot. ch 2, and sl st in 2nd ch from hook. sl st in 2nd and 1st ch of ch 4. sc in same hdc as last sc. 2 sc in each of 3 hdc. sc in 1 hdc, and sl st in 1 hdc. Fasten off; weave in ends.

75 Butterfly

Finished height: 2³⁄₈ in (60 mm)

Thread required: 8 yds (7.3 m)

Body: ch 12. Starting in 3rd ch from hook, sc in 9 ch. 5 sc in 1 ch (at end). Continuing down other side of chain, sc in 10 ch. ch 4, and sl st in 2nd ch from hook to form picot. ch 2. Skip ch 2 space, and sl st in 2 sc.

Right Wings, Row 1: ch 4. tr in next sc. ch 4, and sl st in 2 sc. ch 4, and tr in 1 sc. ch 4 and sl st in 1 sc. Turn.

Right Wings, Row 2: ch 22, and sl st in 18th ch from hook to form loop. sc in next tr. ch 14, and sl st in 14th ch from hook. sc in same tr. ch 12, and sl st in 12th ch from hook. ch 4. Skip ch 4 space, and skip 1 sl st. sl st in next sl st (between wings). ch 14, and sl st in 10th ch from hook. sc in next tr. ch 10, sl st in 10th ch from hook. sc in same tr. ch 10, and sl st in 10th ch from hook. ch 4. Skip ch 4 space, and sl st in sl st. Turn.

Right Wings, Row 3: ch 1. 3 sc in ch 4 space. 6 sc in ch 10 loop. 3 sc in next ch 10 loop. 6 sc in next ch 10 loop. 3 sc in ch 4 space, sl st in sl st (between wings), and 3 sc in ch 4 space. 7 sc in ch 12 loop, and 5 sc in ch 14 loop. In the ch 18 loop: [sc, hdc, 2 dc, ch 2, dc, hdc, 9 sc]. 5 sc in ch 4 space.

Head: Back on body, sl st in next 10 sc.

Left Wings, Row 1: ch 4. tr in next sc. ch 4, and sl st in 2 sc. ch 4, and tr in 1 sc. ch 4 and sl st in 1 sc. Turn.

Left Wings, Row 2: ch 14, and sl st in 10th ch from hook to form loop. sc in next tr. ch 10, and sl st in 10th ch from hook. sc in same tr. ch 10, and sl st in 10th ch from hook. ch 4. sl st in next sl st (between wings). ch 16, and sl st in 12th ch from hook. sc in next tr. ch 14, and sl st in 14th ch from hook. sc in same tr. ch 18, and sl st in 18th ch from hook. ch 4. sl st in next sl st. Turn.

Left Wings, Row 3: ch 1. 5 sc in ch 4 space. In ch 18 loop: [9 sc, hdc, dc, ch 2, 2 dc, hdc, sc]. 5 sc in ch 14 loop, and 7 sc in ch 12 loop. 3 sc in ch 4 space, sl st in sl st (between wings), and 3 sc in next ch 4 space. 6 sc in ch 10 loop, 3 sc in next loop, and 6 sc in the following loop. 3 sc in ch 4 space. sl st in next sc. Fasten off; weave in ends.

Antennae: Cut a length of thread of approximately 3 in (76 mm). Using a needle or crochet hook, draw it through the 2nd sl st of the head, and back through the 4th sl st of the head. Pull through until loose ends are of equal length. Anchor each end by using it to work a single sl st in the same sl st, and fastening off. Trim ends if necessary.

○ = ch   • = sl st   + = sc   ├── = hdc   ├─/ = dc   ├─// = tr   ⟋•▸ = sewn-on antennae

3 The Projects

This chapter presents a selection of ideas to inspire and encourage you to use the featured designs in a variety of ways—on their own, grouped, or joined together.

Tote Bag

Personalize a canvas tote bag with decorative appliques in the theme and colors of your choice. Motifs used here: Flower with Stem (page 55), Water Lily (page 98), Chrysanthemum (page 52), and Garden Hexagon (page 96).

Doilies

Dress up your table with lacy doilies. One of the doilies pictured is a single large motif; the others were made by joining seven identical hexagons. Motifs used here: Scallop-edged Doily (page 94), Flowering Hexagon (page 75), Swirled Hexagon (page 76), and Sunflower Hexagon (page 77).

Lavender Bags

Combine the patterns and textures of crocheted lace with the beautiful smell of lavender, by using lace motifs to decorate dried lavender bags. Motif used here: Serrated Medallion (page 71).

Child's Dress
Ornament a little girl's special dress with an arrangement of her favorite bright appliques. Motifs used here: Dragonfly (page 57) and Butterfly (page 115).

Embellished Collar

Sew small motifs to a plain blouse
to create delicate collar accents.
Motif used here: Tiny Heart (page 52).

Scarf

Join square motifs to form a gorgeous,
one-of-a-kind scarf. Use fine cotton thread
for a lacy scarf like the one pictured,
or substitute a heavier yarn to make a
cozy winter accessory. Motifs used here:
Daisy-centered Square (page 63) and
Floating-flower Square (page 90).

Index

Credits

Dedication
I'd like to dedicate this book in memory of my grandmothers. Anna Foley was a prolific crocheter, whose large, warm afghans I remember fondly, and Muriel Watson was a specialist in the clever, the crafty, and the colorful. To this day, their craftsmanship inspires my own.

Acknowledgments
I'm grateful to my family for both their support and their patience, and to my friends at Quarto for all their help and encouragement.

Many thanks to Coats & Clark for supplying the Aunt Lydia's thread.

Yarns used
The motifs in this book were made using one of the following brands of thread and in one of the colors listed below:

Aunt Lydia's, by Coats & Clark (www.shopredheart.com)
Natural, Maize, Goldenrod, Orchid Pink, French Rose, Victory Red, Wood Violet, Bridal Blue, Delft, Mint Green, Frosty Green, Silver

Lizbeth, by Handy Hands (www.hhtatting.com)
Mocha Brown Lt., Purple Iris Lt., Country Turquoise Lt., Seagreen Lt., Leaf Green Lt.